Intelligent Design:
An Intellectual Challenge?

Maziar H. Etemadi and Peter Øhrstrøm (eds.)

AALBORG UNIVERSITY PRESS

Cover photo courtesy of "Den Virtuella Floran, Naturhistoriska riksmuseet, Stockholm."

Intelligent Design: An Intellectual Challenge?
Edited by Maziar H. Etemadi and Peter Øhrstrøm

© The Authors and Aalborg University Press, 2007
Cover: Henrik Schärfe
Layout: Ulrik Sandborg-Petersen
Printed by Publizon A/S
ISBN: 978-87-7307-930-0

Distribution:
Aalborg University Press
Niels Jernes Vej 6B
9220 Aalborg
Denmark
Phone: (+45) 96 35 71 40, Fax: (+45) 96 35 00 76
E-mail: aauf@forlag.aau.dk
www.forlag.aau.dk

All rights reserved. No part of this book may be reprinted or reproduced or utilized in any form or by any electronic, mechanical, or other means, now known or hereafter invented, including photocopying and recording, or in any information storage or retrieval system, without permission in writing from the publishers, except for reviews and short excerpts in scholarly publications.

Contents

1 Intelligent Design in Historical Perspective   7
   1.1 The Logical Foundation of Science 10
   1.2 The Pioneers of Natural Science and the Belief in Intelligent Design 13
   1.3 The Rejection of the Idea of Nature as Designed 15
   1.4 The Anthropic Principle and the Reintroduced Idea of Design   16
   1.5 Design, Purpose and Scientific Discourse 19
   1.6 Conclusion 20

2 The Basic Ideas of Intelligent Design   21
   2.1 What ID is not 22
   2.2 What ID is 22
   2.3 The Context: Scientific Materialism 23
   2.4 Hanging in Midair 24
   2.5 Nature Strikes Back 25
   2.6 A "Local Fine Tuning" Argument 25
   2.7 ID in Biology 30
   2.8 Saint Darwin 32
   2.9 Starting to Stick 34

3 Evolution or Intelligent Design   37
   3.1 The Question: The Rationality of the Argument 38
   3.2 The Inference from Design to a Designer 42
   3.3 The identification of intelligence 46
   3.4 Intelligence and design models 48
   3.5 The Role of Purpose 50
   3.6 Evolution versus Design 52
   3.7 The Natural Constants 55
   3.8 The inclusive concept of the world 58
   3.9 Creation of the world — intelligently designed by human beings   59

4	**The designed water flow through a plant leaf**	**63**
	4.1 Introduction	63
	4.2 Physical principles	65
	4.3 The porous medium model of a leaf	66
	4.4 The circular leaf	71
	4.5 The holism of an elliptic problem	72
	4.6 Computations of theoretical leaves	75
	4.7 Conclusions	76
5	**To be or not to be intelligently designed – that's the question**	**81**
	5.1 Are there absolute, immutable proofs that God does exist?	82
	5.2 My metaphysical argument against intelligent design – the evolutionary alarm clock	86
	5.3 My epistemological argument against intelligent design	89
	5.4 The confusion of meaning and truth	93
6	**Evolution, Intelligent Design and the re-emergence of Militant Atheism**	**99**
	6.1 The Dawkins and Dennett arguments	101
	6.2 The intellectual *superbia* of Dawkins and Dennett	104
	6.3 Intelligent Design and religious belief	105
	6.4 Turning the table	108
	6.5 Conclusion	109

Introduction

On May 16, 2006, the *Centre for Philosophy and Science Studies* at Aalborg University hosted an international seminar on intelligent design. During the seminar the ideas of intelligent design were carefully and critically discussed. This book is the result of the work presented at the seminar and the subsequent discussions on the topics raised at the seminar.

The basic claim of intelligent design is that some significant problems inherent in the core of the scientific theories about the origin of life are being neglected in the mainstream of modern epistemology, scientific thinking, and philosophy of science. The advocates of intelligent design hold that certain features of the universe and of living things can only be explained by an intelligent cause, not just be reference to an undirected process such as natural selection. They also hold that a proper description of nature should include the notion of 'purpose' i.e. that teleological descriptions should not in principle be excluded from the scientific literature. A great majority of the scientific community rejects the scientific validity and relevance of the claims of intelligent design, which they characterize as non-serious and at least semi-religious. It is also claimed that intelligent design is based on a certain reactionary political agenda. On the other hand, regardless of the motivations and political ambitions of the founders and defenders of the idea of intelligent design, this idea has given rise to some interesting epistemological, methodological, and ontological problems, which are relevant for the formulation and understanding of science. This has also made it essential to discuss basic ideas within the philosophy of nature and the philosophy of science, not only in a technical manner, but also in a broader perspective.

In this book a group of scientists and philosophers discuss these topics. Some of the authors defend the basic ideas of intelligent design and others oppose these ideas. In some the chapters of this book the attempt has been to focus on the historical and epistemological aspects of the debate. Perhaps the most important result from the seminar and subsequent discussions is the identification of some crucial challenges and problems regarding the understanding of the scientific approach to reality and the basic assumptions of epistemology.

Maziar Etemadi & Peter Øhrstrøm

Chapter 1

Intelligent Design in Historical Perspective

Peter Øhrstrøm
Center for Philosophy and Science Studies
Aalborg University
Denmark

Steinar Thorvaldsen
Section for Informatics
Tromsø University College
Norway

The advocates of intelligent design hold that important properties or aspects of nature are intended, i.e., that they are the results of intelligent planning and design. In other words, they maintain that some features of cosmos and nature (i.e., the physical universe and the living things) are caused by non-human intelligence. Nothing in particular is said about the nature of the designer. However, it is clear that most advocates of intelligent design imagine a transcendent designer and not some other sort of extra-terrestrial intelligence. In this way, the position is mainly related to the various religious beliefs according to which the universe is conceived as the outcome of divine intention.

The very notion of 'design', however, certainly needs some further clarification. According to Del Ratzsch[1], a design is "a deliberately intended or produced pattern", and he adds that a pattern may be understood as "an abstract structure which correlates in special ways to mind or is *mind correlative*" in such a way that the structure "fits human processes of cognition" or "makes sense to humans". This means that a design is not just any order in nature. To be a design it has to be a pattern which is there because of a plan or intent, and which has been realized in the physical world.

The claim of intelligent design is not that everything in the universe is designed or planned. It is consistent with the view that certain aspects of nature are caused by stochastic processes in nature. The claim of intelligent design is merely that a number of initial conditions and essential properties of cosmos and nature are in fact planned or designed intelligently. The main argument of the advocates of intelligent design is that there are some very complex structures in nature, which cannot be satisfactorily explained as the result of natural processes. As pointed out by Howard J. van Till, proponents of Intelligent Design have argued that "there is empirical evidence that the universe's system of natural capabilities for forming things is inadequate for assembling certain information-rich biological structures"[2]. It could be added that similar claims have been made regarding very complex patterns in physics and cosmology. For this reason the advocates of intelligent design have maintained that a proper and satisfactory description of cosmos and nature should include references to 'purpose', i.e. that, in principle, teleological descriptions should not in principle be excluded from the scientific literature.

A great majority of the scientific community rejects the scientific validity and relevance of the ideas of intelligent design. Some writers have even claimed that these ideas are scientifically dangerous, since a conclusion such as 'it is designed' in their opinion is likely to block further inquiry into the topics in question. In many cases, the ideas of intelligent design have been characterized as non-serious, at least when presented as scientifically relevant descriptions of cosmos and nature. Instead, intelligent design has been viewed as based on various religious beliefs and on a certain reactionary political agenda.

Intelligent design has sometimes been presented as a new view invented in the 1990s by ultra-rightwing fundamentalists in USA. However, although it is true that a new intelligent design movement has become very strong and that it has been intensely debated in USA and in other parts of the world since the mid 1990s, and although it is probably true that some of the founders and defenders of the ideas of intelligent design have related their interests in these ideas to

---

[1] Ratzsch (2001, p. 3).
[2] van Till (2003).

their ideological and political ambitions, it would be a severe mistake to see the idea of plan and design in the physical and biological world as something brand new invented in the 1990s in USA. The basic idea of nature and cosmos as being intended is definitely not new. On the contrary, the view that essential characteristics of cosmos and nature are results of planning rather than chance or accidents is very old. In this paper, we are going to argue that this view was essential in the process that led to the rise of modern science.

In a letter to J.E. Switzer, written in 1953, Albert Einstein stated that modern science presupposes

1. The invention of formal logical systems, and

2. The discovery of the possibility of finding out causal relationships by systematic experiment.[3]

The former invention was made by Aristotle and further developed by later ancient and medieval philosophers working in the Aristotelian tradition, whereas scientists discovered the latter during the Renaissance.

Einstein's analysis is obviously true, and it can be added that both prerequisites of modern science should be understood in the context of design and transcendence.

In section one of this paper, we shall show that the tradition of logical investigation, on which scientific inquiry as such is based, is itself strongly related to the belief in transcendence according to which it is quite natural to look for order, plan and design in the world. In section two, it will be argued that the important pioneers of modern science in general maintained that the world was planned and designed by God, and that this view stimulated rather than stopped their scientific investigations. The reaction during the 18th and 19th centuries against the universe as designed will be discussed in section three, whereas the modern opening established through the anthropic principle for reintroducing the idea of design in the scientific discourse will be considered in section four. Finally, in section five, we shall briefly discuss the possible rôle of the vocabulary suggested by the advocates of intelligent design in future scientific discourse and also some of the problems which the modern movement of intelligent design has to face.

---

[3] See Needham (1969, p. 43).

1.1 The Logical Foundation of Science

It is commonly agreed that Aristotle was the founding father of Western logic, although elements of logic can certainly be shown to be present in pre-Socratic thought and in the writings of Plato.

One of the basic concepts in Aristotle's approach to logic was the syllogism. In fact, his system of the valid syllogisms can be understood as the first axiomatic system ever. Aristotle argued that the set of the valid syllogisms can be organized in a beautiful deductive system. However, this obviously presupposes that the valid syllogisms are known. But which of the many possible syllogisms are valid and which are not? Aristotle provided a very clear answer to this question. In fact, it is most interesting that it is possible in any group of people to reach a very high degree of agreement on the question of validity of the syllogisms. For instance, everybody will agree that the syllogism:

> some S are M
> all M are P
> ergo: some S are P

is valid whereas everybody will agree that the structure

> some S are M
> some M are P
> ergo: some S are P

is certainly not a valid syllogism. But what is the origin of this agreement? The same fundamental question could be asked with respect to many other kinds of logical reasoning. Aristotle himself formulated the question in a very precise way:

> And the starting-point of reason is not reason but something superior to reason. What, then, could be superior even to knowledge and to intellect, except God?[4]

Aristotle obviously considered the origin of logic to be transcendent and 'super-intelligent'. Although he did not present any detailed exposition of the nature of logic, he was obviously aware of the fact that the question of validity of logical arguments is related to the problem of the semantic structures of natural language. His interest in language and semantics becomes evident when one considers his famous ten categories, which can be used in order to explain

---
[4] Aristotle (n.d., Book 8, Section 1248a27-28).

the meaning of a sentence. The categories can be viewed as basic components of meaning. The very fact that we are able to understand and to reason about essential elements of the world may lead us to believe in a transcendent designer. That was at least the way things were conceived in the mainstream of scholastic interpretation of Aristotelian thought.

One of the most important scholars in the medieval tradition was Thomas Aquinas (1224-74), who suggested five ways to God based on reflection and reasoning about the world. In the present context, the most important argument is the fifth way, which is now seen as the classical argument from design. It may be described in the following manner:

> The Fifth way starts from the orderly character of the mundane events, argues that all things are directed toward one end (the principle of finality), and concludes that this universal order points to the existence of an Orderer of all things.[5]

According to Thomas, this 'Orderer of all things' is the Christian God, the Creator. This conclusion is not part of the argument from design as such. However, following the scholastic (and Aristotelian) line of thinking, man's capability of logic and rationality as well as the validity of logic and rationality as such must come from something superior, something or someone transcendent. Much later, C.S. Peirce (1839-1914) tried to answer a similar question: How can it be that man using scientific investigation relatively effectively can discover important aspects of the truth about nature? In answering questions like that he formulated what he called 'A Neglected Argument for the Reality of God', which was first published in the Hibbert Journal (1908). Peirce rejected the idea that the scientific results have come about only "by some such modification of chance as the Darwinian supposes" (CP 6.476). To Peirce, this was simply too unrealistic. It seemed obvious to him that man has done much better than that during the history of science. Peirce formulated his own answer in the following way:

> There is a reason, an interpretation, a logic, in the course of scientific advance, and this indisputably proves to him who has perceptions of rational or significant relations, that man's mind must have been attuned to the truth of things in order to discover what he has discovered. It is the very bedrock of logical truth. (CP 6.476)

---

[5]Bourke (1967, p. 110).

Peirce's idea is that man has been created with a special kind of mind, which makes him able to discover truth. For Peirce, this view was intimately related to his belief in God, according to which man may even "see" God, if he opens his eyes and heart! (CP 6.493)

A similar reflection on man's ability to find truth can be found in the writings of the great Polish logician Jan Łukasiewicz (1878-1956), who beautifully formulated his view in the following way:

> Now, whenever I work even on the least significant logistic problem, for instance, when I search for the shortest axiom of the implicational propositional calculus I always have the impression that I am facing a powerful, most coherent and most resistant structure. I sense that structure as if it were a concrete, tangible object, made of the hardest metal, a hundred times stronger than steel and concrete. I cannot change anything in it; I do not create anything of my own will, but by strenuous work I discover in it ever new details and arrive at unshakable and eternal truths. Where is and what is that ideal structure? A believer would say that it is in God and is His thought.[6]

This view is very close to the traditional Christian view: Given the belief in a rational God and the belief that man is created in the image of God, it becomes natural and reasonable to understand the logical structure of reality as an essential aspect of the designed order of the created universe, i.e., as a reflection of the divine wisdom. In fact, a similar view of a cosmic rationality and wisdom much deeper than the positivistic approach to reason has recently been strongly defended by Pope Benedikt XVI:

> Modern scientific reason quite simply has to accept the rational structure of matter and the correspondence between our spirit and the prevailing rational structures of nature as a given, on which its methodology has to be based.[7]

If the Pope is right, the belief in a rational world order is essential for science as such. This view seems very convincing. Without a belief in a structure or design in the physical universe, many scientists will probably lose their motivation. As we shall see in the next section, a strong belief in the rational structure of the physical universe was a very important background for the rise of modern science.

---

[6]Łukasiewicz (1970, p. 249).
[7]Pope Benedict XVI (2006).

1.2 The Pioneers of Natural Science and the Belief in Intelligent Design

The history of science is very long, but the scientific idea of establishing causal relationships by systematic experiments is relatively recent. It was invented in Europe during the Renaissance and it turned out to be essential to what we now call natural science. But why was this invention not made in India or in China? In many respects, these civilisations in the East were more advanced than the European civilisation in the 16th century. According to J. Needham, this should be explained referring to the rather different approaches to nature in Europe and in the civilisations in the East:

> (In China) ... there was no confidence that the code of Nature's laws could ever be unveiled and read, because there was no assurance that a divine being, even more rational than ourselves, had ever formulated such a code capable of being read.[8]

If Needham is right, it would also be correct to say that the rise of modern science is at least partly based on the belief in some sort of intelligent design in nature. As it has been argued elsewhere[9], the pioneers of natural science saw the very fact that we may gain reliable and meaningful information about reality from our senses and our reason as an indication of some kind of divine order and design in nature. One may say that this is how the pioneers of natural science understood why understanding is possible at all. One interesting example would be Johannes Kepler (1571-1630) who believed that man could acknowledge the mathematical order in the universe. In a letter to Mästerlin, April 19, 1597, he wrote:

> Those laws [which govern the material world] lie within the power of understanding of the human mind; God wanted us to perceive them when He created us in His image in order that we may take part in His own thoughts...[10]

Kepler maintained that since man is created in the image of God, the human mind is at least to some extent in fact capable of understanding the divine rationality and design expressed in nature. It seems that Kepler's view can meaningfully be explained in terms of the diagram in Figure 1.1.

---

[8]Needham (1969, p. 327).
[9]See, e.g., Thorvaldsen (2003).
[10]Caspar and Dyck (1930, Band I, p. 44).

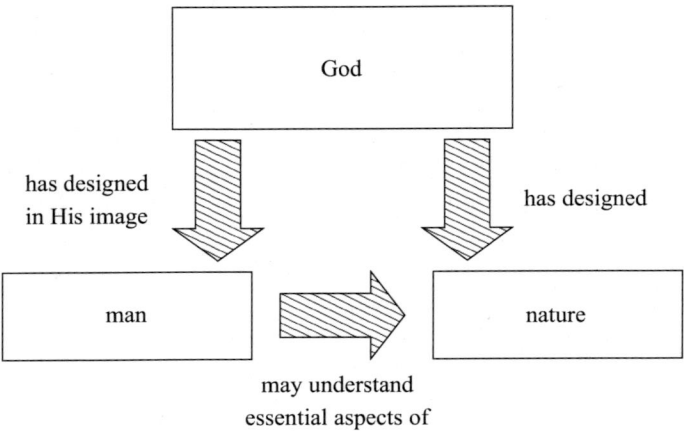

Figure 1.1: Diagram of Kepler's view.

According to this view, God has created the physical world giving form, design and structure in accordance with certain mathematical and logical ideas. In addition, God has created man with the capability of understanding this mathematical and logical code according to which the physical universe has been structured. A similar view can be found in the writings of Galileo Galilei (1564-1643):

> Philosophy is written in that great book which ever lies before our eyes — I mean the universe — but we cannot understand it if we do not first learn the language and grasp the symbols, in which it is written. This book is written in the mathematical language ... [11]

Obviously, the idea of the universe as similar to a book presupposes the view that important patterns of the universe are intended, i.e., designed. Galilei did not claim that we as human beings will be able to read all the parts of "that great book", but to the extent that we can understand its language we may understand essential parts of the divine wisdom expressed in the physical universe.

The view of the universe as intended by God in his wisdom was basically common to all the important pioneers of modern science. Like Isaac Newton (1642-1727), they all believed that the universe is intended, created, and

---

[11] Drake (1957, p. 237).

ruled by God who is understood as a living, intelligent, powerful, and supreme being.[12]

1.3 The Rejection of the Idea of Nature as Designed

During the 18th century, it became important for many writers to make a distinction between science and religion. This was among others the view of Immanuel Kant (1724-1804). He had clear objections to the classical argument from design. On the other hand, in his *Critique of Practical Reason* (1788) he wrote:

> Two things fill the mind with ever new and increasing admiration and awe, the more often and steadily we reflect upon them: the starry heavens above me and the moral law within me.[13]

This at least suggests that he was sensitive to the kind of observations which have led people to the belief in the world as intended.

During the 19th and 20th centuries, the belief in the universe as designed became less influential. Many scientists and philosophers wanted to have a worldview without any direct or indirect reference to a divine creator. Charles Darwin was one of the most famous scientists who gave up his belief in a divine designer. In his autobiography, he wrote:

> The old argument from design in nature as given by Paley, which formerly seemed to me so conclusive, fails, now that the law of natural selection has been discovered.[14]

It seems, however, that one of Darwin's main reasons for giving up his former belief in God was based on considerations regarding the problem of evil, i.e., not a strictly scientific reason. In his own words:

> I cannot persuade myself that a beneficent and omnipotent God would have designedly created the Ichneumonidae with the express intention of their feeding within the bodies of Caterpillars, or that a cat should play with mice.[15]

---

[12] See Thorvaldsen (2003, p. 27).
[13] Quoted from Schönfeld (2003).
[14] Quoted from Nancy (1998, p. 84).
[15] Quoted from Nancy (1998, p. 90-91).

It has in fact often been the case that various — not scientific, but rather philosophical or existential — reasons have been given for rejecting the idea of divine designer of nature.

The replacement of the design idea has been some sort of mythology dealing with the notion of chance. One of the strong claims regarding this view has been made by Jacque Monod in his *Chance and Necessity* (1971):

> Man at last knows that he is alone in the unfeeling immensity of the universe, of which he has emerged only by chance. Neither his destiny nor his duty has been written down.[16]

It has become an essential part of this new paradigm to exclude all references to 'purpose' and teleological explanations in general from scientific discourse. As stated by one of the famous advocates of this view, G.G. Simpson, even man should be conceived as 'purposeless':

> The meaning of evolution is that man is the result of a purposeless and materialistic process that did not have him in mind.[17]

Following this line of thought it has been important to most scientific writers to avoid all references to 'purpose' in nature. The physical and biological world has in general been conceived as 'purposeless'. Until recently, this kind of very strong 'teleophobia' — in fact almost a teleology taboo — has dominated scientific circles, i.e., there has been a clear reaction among scientists against any reference to purpose in nature. On the other hand, some well known scientists have maintained that we still need to explain why so many elements and aspects of nature at least appear to be designed, and they have argued that this can only be done using ideas of "a new kind of science"[18].

1.4 The Anthropic Principle and the Reintroduced Idea of Design

During the 1980s, it became evident that an expanding universe must have some very specific properties at its beginning if it is going to include biological life at some later stage of its history. In 1986, the scientists John D. Barrow and Frank J. Tipler published their very influential book, *The Anthropic Cosmological Principle*, in which they discussed the interpretation of the fact that

---

[16] Monod (1971, p. 167).
[17] Simpson (1953, p. 179).
[18] Wolfram (2002, p. 861).

the universe at its beginning had these very rare properties which would allow biological life (including man) to exist at some later stage of its history. It is outside the scope of this paper to give a detailed account of the many different versions of the anthropic principle discussed by Barrow and Tipler – and later also by others. But it should be noted that in their book, Barrow and Tipler suggested a clear relation between their findings and the long tradition of dealing with teleological explanations. One of the principles which they considered in their book was the socalled 'strong anthropic principle':

> There exists one possible Universe 'designed' with the goal of generating and sustaining 'observers.'[19]

The interesting point here is, of course, the use of the word 'designed'. In a sense, the authors are here breaking the teleology taboo. The idea seems to be that if a designer at the beginning of the universe wanted to make sure that biological (including intelligent) life could exist at a later stage of the history of the universe, he would have to make sure that the laws of nature work in a certain way and that the fundamental constants of nature have certain rather specific values.

The need for very special conditions at the beginning of the expanding universe is a rather established insight. As the theoretical physicist Paul Davies has put it in his book *The Cosmic Blueprint*[20]:

> The really amazing thing is not that life on Earth is balanced on a knife-edge, but that the entire universe is balanced on a knife-edge, and would be total chaos if any of the natural constants were off even slightly. You see, even if you dismiss man as a chance happening, the fact remains that the universe seems unreasonably suited to the existence of life — almost contrived — you might say a put-up job.[21]

And Davies adds:

> I hope the foregoing discussion will have convinced the reader that the natural world is not just any old concoction of entities and forces, but a marvellously ingenious and unified mathematical scheme ... these rules look as if they are the product of intelligent design. I do not see how that can be denied.[22]

---

[19] Barrow and Tipler (1986, p. 22).
[20] Davies (1988).
[21] Quoted from Bossard (2005).
[22] Quoted from Bossard (2005).

However, although the properties of the universe may look as if they are the product of intelligent design, they do not have to be exactly that. Other interpretations are possible. One alternative possibility would be the so-called multiverse-hypothesis, i.e., the idea that there is not only one universe, but in fact infinitely many universes with all kinds of different properties. According to this view, we live in one of these parallel universes, which will of course be one with the properties suited for biological life. Paul Davies has made the following comment on this idea:

> To postulate an infinity of unseen and unseeable universes just to explain the one we do see seems like a case of excess baggage carried to the extreme. It is simpler to postulate one unseen God.[23]

Although, this criticism of the multiverse-hypothesis sounds very reasonable, it does not finally settle the questions regarding the interpretation of the facts which have given rise to the various anthropic principles. These interpretation questions are still open, and they may in fact be undecidable from a logical point of view. What is important in the present context, however, is that the discussions regarding the anthropic principles have made it acceptable to include teleological explanations in the scientific discourse. In other words, the discussion regarding the anthropic principles has made it possible for scientists to reintroduce design notions in various scientific contexts.

It should, however, be added that it is possible to make a distinction between the use of teleological explanations and concepts in the context of fundamental cosmology and the use of the same explanations and concepts within biology. It seems that Paul Davies is ready to accept the idea of the laws and natural constants being designed, whereas he refuses the idea of the miraculous intervention of a divine designer in the course of time. In his own words:

> There is no doubt that ... the hypothesis of an intelligent designer applied to the laws of nature is far superior than the designer ... who violates the laws of nature from time to time by working miracles in the evolutionary history. Design-by-laws is incomparably more intelligent than design-by-miracles.[24]

When formulated in this way, Davies' reaction is quite understandable. Why should a transcendent designer want to violate his own laws? But maybe the problem lies in the very notion of 'law of nature'. Again, we may refer

---

[23] Quoted from Bossard (2005).
[24] Davies (2006, p. 226).

to C.S. Peirce, according to whom the traditional notion of a 'law of nature' should be conceived as a "course of nature" or a "habit of nature". For this reason Peirce would not see miracles as violations of laws of nature but as special and important events in history.[25]

1.5 Design, Purpose and Scientific Discourse

Given the impact of the debate regarding the anthropic principles and the present discussions regarding intelligent design, it becomes relevant to discuss whether notions of design should again be allowed in scientific theories and descriptions. As mentioned above, most scientists are still against including such notions in the scientific discourse. As mentioned, some scientists even fear that the use of teleological explanations in science is likely to block further inquiry into the topics in question. However, given the historical background, it would definitely be a misunderstanding to assume that the use of teleological explanations as such will be dangerous in science and that we therefore should ban all references to 'plan', 'design', and 'purpose' from serious scientific discussions on the features of cosmos and nature. The use of such references has never been a hindrance to scientific progress, and there is no reason to believe that it should function in that way now if accepted in scientific theory and vocabulary.

Allowing teleological explanations and the formulation of scientific problems referring to 'purpose' and 'design' will obviously broaden the scientific discourse. And it should be added that an extended language will bring us back to the basic scientific language used by the pioneers of modern science. There is no reason to exclude the possibility that a wider scientific language may lead to new questions and new ideas, which may in turn give rise to new findings in science. A similar view has been defended by Owen Gingerich, who is a Harward professor of astronomy and the history of science, in his fascinating paper: "Dare a Scientist Believe in Design?":

> So, while I differ from those Christian biochemists who postulate some new kind of "origin science", I do think a science totally devoid of the idea of design may be in danger of running into a blank wall. And this brings me to ask again, is the idea of design a threat to science? And I answer no, perhaps design might even be a necessary ingredient in science.[26]

---

[25] See O'Hara (forthcoming, p. 14).
[26] Gingerich (1994, p. 31-2).

However, there are still many questions which should be discussed in relation to the question of reintroducing notions of 'plan' and 'design' in scientific discourse. As pointed out by Paul Davies, one of the difficult notions which need further clarification is the idea of cosmological design prior to time itself.[27]

1.6 Conclusion

As we have argued, the pioneers of modern science used teleological explanations as well as ideas of design and plan in their scientific discourse. We have also seen that such explanations and ideas became banned in scientific texts during the following period, and that some scientists and philosophers of science have recently argued that notions of design etc. should be accepted again in science. Since the publication of Barrow and Tipler's book in 1986, it has often been argued that the anthropic principles can only be discussed in a satisfactory manner if teleological explanations and concepts are accepted in the discussion. Recently, advocates of intelligent design have made similar claims. Of course, such questions will also be tied up with the ambition to give a true account of nature. As pointed out by Pope Benedikt XVI in his recent lecture in Regensburg, honest scientists who treasure scientific ethos will always want "to be obedient to the truth". If the advocates of intelligent design are right, scientific truth cannot be fully accounted for without accepting teleological ingredients in the scientific language. If they are wrong, all cases of apparent purpose and design in nature are in fact nothing more than apparent, and are definitely not signs of any real intention or plan. From a strictly scientific point of view, however, it may formally and empirically be both undecidable and unknowable who is in fact right and who is wrong.[28] The matter ultimately has to be decided on the basis of metaphysical and other philosophical arguments. This obviously does not make the discussion between the positions uninteresting or unimportant.

---

[27] See Davies (2006, p. 227 ff.).
[28] Yockey (2005, p. 171-175).

Chapter 2

The Basic Ideas of Intelligent Design

Jay W. Richards
Research Fellow
Acton Institute
Grand Rapids, Michigan

Anyone who reads newspapers and listens to television news, especially in the United States, has heard something about "intelligent design" (ID) and the "intelligent design movement." The debate about intelligent design has gotten a great deal of coverage in the US, but it is increasingly being discussed in Europe as well. Unfortunately, media portrayals of intelligent design almost inevitably misrepresent it.

In the US, the media script is so uniform, that I've wondered if every reporter uses a pre-programmed computer macro. Whether in New York, Los Angeles, Darby, Montana, or Dover, Pennsylvania, the reporter just types "control-alt-Scopes Trope". Out pops the witty headline: "Creationism Evolves." Then there's the opening, with predictable reference to the infamous Scopes Monkey Trial in Dayton, Tennessee, in 1925. Fundamentalists slug it out with scientists over Darwin's theory of evolution. Science loses. Then there are some sentences about the contemporary religious right and its desire to put the Bible in the science class as the first step toward establishing a theocracy. Next comes a quote representing the view of all scientists, with the phrase "overwhelming evidence." And then, finally, inevitably, we get a quote from some Elmer Gantry character as a stand in for anyone who questions "evolution" (a word often invoked but rarely defined). The rest of the story practically writes itself.

Of course, the media are simply following the uncharitable interpretation of ID of its leading academic critics. Unfortunately, that interpretation keeps readers from understanding what ID is really about. In what follows, I will not attempt to develop a detailed argument for intelligent design, but rather to explain what ID is, and what it is not.

2.1 What ID is not

Since most people who have heard of ID have misconceptions about it, let's start by considering what ID is not.

1. ID is not creationism. It may have religious *implications*, but it does not require religious *premises*.

2. ID is not natural theology.

3. ID doesn't uniquely identify a designer.

4. ID is not the argument that because something is so complex, God must have done it.

5. ID is not a Christian plot to outlaw the teaching of evolution in public schools or to establish a theocracy.

2.2 What ID is

But rather than belaboring these points, I would like to explain what intelligent design is. Although there are now many different ID arguments from a variety of scientific disciplines presented in articles, books, and even television documentaries, all of these arguments can be boiled down to two basic claims:

1. We can detect the activities of intelligent agents on the basis of certain types of evidence.

2. Such evidence exists in the natural world and can be detected.

The first claim is surely uncontroversial. We all detect the activities of intelligence all the time. And, except in the case of introspection, we never observe or experience agents directly. We know what other agents do by their effects. You are detecting an intelligent agent (I hope) by reading this text. You detect agency when you listen to music, or read a novel, or view a sculpture. You do it countless times everyday, and for the most part, you do it accurately.

The second claim, of course, is more controversial. But surely there's no problem with it in principle. If activities of intelligent agency are detectable, for example, because they produce certain types of patterns, then surely it's a factual question as to whether such patterns exist in the natural world. So, as a "theory," ID is a theory of design detection intended for use on the evidence of nature. As a community, ID is a diverse and interdisciplinary research program of scientists, philosophers, and other scholars who are interested in discovering and studying patterns in nature that are best explained as the result of intelligent causes, and developing testable arguments based on such patterns. Looking at publicly available scientific evidence, ID theorists seek to answer the question: "Does nature display objective evidence of design or purpose?"

2.3 The Context: Scientific Materialism

To understand the debate over intelligent design, you also need to keep in mind (1) the role of scientific materialism in dictating what can be considered, (2) the changing state of the scientific evidence, and (3) a distinction: the difference between evidence against a prevailing theory, and positive evidence in favor of intelligent design. If you get these points, you'll understand more about the current debate over intelligent design than most of its critics and 90% of the mainstream media.

First, scientific materialism. Let's pick up the story in the nineteenth century. Natural science in the Victorian Age, or rather, its materialistic gloss, offered a simple view of the universe. (1) The universe has always existed, and so we need not address where it came from. (2) Everything in the universe, large and small, submits to a few well understood, deterministic laws. (3) Life turned up as a result of luck and chemistry. (3) Cells, for their part, are basically little blobs of Jell-O. And (4) those complicated adaptations of organisms result from a starkly simple process called natural selection: this almost miraculously creative process seizes and passes along those minor, random variations within a population that provide a survival advantage. (In the twentieth century, those minor variations were identified with random genetic mutations. This is called *Neo*-Darwinism.) That's it.

As I said, that's a gloss, an interpretation of science. That gloss is called scientific materialism: there is one god, matter, and science is its prophet. For a doctrinal statement of this worldview, there's none better than the opening line from Carl Sagan's famous *Cosmos* series: "The Cosmos is all that is, or ever was, or ever will be."[1]

2.4 Hanging in Midair

This materialistic story was buttressed by a philosophical movement called positivism. Positivists sought to reduce science and knowledge to sense data. They had an axe to grind. They wanted to purge "metaphysics" from science and from the public sphere generally. Metaphysics included all moral judgments and certainly all religious claims involving beings that were not directly experienced by the senses.

Positivism, alas, suffered several terminal illnesses. Perhaps the most severe one was this: positivists claimed that only statements that can be verified by the senses are meaningful or at least scientific. That statement, however, cannot itself be verified by the senses. So, by its own accounting, the central thesis of positivism was meaningless or at least "unscientific."

The positivists made several attempts to save the patient. But their cure was worse than the disease: any criterion liberal enough to avoid contradiction and accommodate actual scientific practice let "metaphysics" in as well. Such problems eventually led to the demise of the entire positivist enterprise. In the end, some positivists even confessed their sins. For instance, in a BBC radio interview, Brian McGee once asked A.J. Ayer, the father of logical positivism, what the main defect of positivism was. The main problem, Ayer said, was that it was "nearly all false."[2]

The collapse of positivism left scientific materialism without a foundation. But among intellectuals and scientists, positivism has lingered on, like the stench of burnt toast in the air. It often appears in the form of an unwritten rule. Scientists, we're told, must not appeal to intelligent agency when trying to explain either the features of the natural world, or the natural world itself. (Such a rule would exclude most of the founders of modern science, including Copernicus, Kepler, and Newton, from the exclusive club of science. But let that pass for now.) According to this tidy rule, anyone who dares speak of purpose or design within science ceases to be a scientist.

---

[1] See Sagan (1993, p. 4).
[2] See McGee (1978, p. 131).

2.5 Nature Strikes Back

But nature apparently didn't realize that it was under an obligation to conform to a narrow definition of science. For as soon as this Procrustean bed was made, the real world began to resist. The startling revelations of the quantum realm suggested that the world was not quite as submissive as many had expected.

Then, in the 1920s, astronomer Edwin Hubble discovered that the light from distant galaxies was "red-shifted." It had stretched during the course of its travels. This suggested that the universe is expanding in every direction. Reversing the process in their minds, scientists were suddenly confronted with the prospect of a universe that had come into existence in the finite past. The universe has an age. Who knew! Hubble's discovery and the confirming evidence that followed flatly contradicted the earlier picture of an eternal and self-existing cosmos. The universe itself had re-introduced the question of its origin to a community that was avoiding the question altogether.

This was just the beginning. In the 1960s and '70s, physicists began to notice that the universal constants of physics, such as the forces of gravity and electromagnetism, seemed to be "finely-tuned" for the existence of complex life. If these constants were much different, or if we were to try to pick their values at random, we would almost always get a universe hostile to life. Even the late astrophysicist Fred Hoyle, one of the founders of the Steady State model and an intransigent atheist, admitted:

A commonsense interpretation of the facts suggests that a superintellect has monkeyed with physics, as well as chemistry and biology, and that there are no blind forces worth speaking about in nature.[3]

2.6 A "Local Fine Tuning" Argument

Still more recently, growing evidence in astronomy has revealed that even in a finely tuned universe, many local things have to go just right to build a single habitable planet. This evidence is part of the foundation of the design argument developed in *The Privileged Planet*,[4] which I co-authored with astronomer Guillermo Gonzalez.

Following an idea inspired by materialism, called the Copernican Principle, most scientists have supposed that our Solar System is typical and that the origin and evolution of life must be quite likely, given the vast size and

---

[3] Hoyle (1982, p. 16).
[4] Gonzalez and Richards (2004).

great age of the universe. Accordingly, most have assumed that the universe is probably teeming not just with life, but complex, intelligent life.

But the scientific evidence has stubbornly pointed in the opposite direction. We're now learning how much must go right to a get a habitable planet. The list gets longer all the time. Complex life in particular probably needs many of the things that we Earthlings enjoy: a rocky terrestrial planet similar in size and composition to the Earth, with plate tectonics to recycle nutrients, and the right kind of atmosphere; a large, well placed moon to contribute to tides and stabilize the tilt of the planet's axis. That planet needs to be just the right distance from the right kind of single star, in a nearly circular orbit—to maintain liquid water on its surface.

It also needs a home within a stable planetary system that includes some outlying giant planets to protect the inner system from too many deadly comet impacts. That planetary system must be nestled in a safe neighborhood in the right kind of galaxy, with enough heavy elements to build terrestrial planets. And that planet will need to form during the narrow habitable window of cosmic history. (This is to say nothing of having a universe with a fine-tuned set of physical laws to make stars, planets, and people possible in the first place. But that's another long and complicated story.)

Since the mid-1990s, astronomers have been able to detect planets around other Sun-like stars. And they have taught us an important, if unadvertised lesson. Planetary systems are not all alike. In fact, mounting evidence suggests that the conditions needed for complex life are exceedingly rare, the probability of them all occurring at the same place and time, minuscule.

So argued Peter Ward and Donald Brownlee in their best-selling book *Rare Earth: Why Complex Life is Uncommon in the Universe*.[5] Ward and Brownlee obviously challenge the letter of the Copernican Principle. But they don't challenge its spirit. Intuitively, you might think that such a precise configuration of life-friendly factors suggests that Earth is part of some cosmic design. Ward and Brownlee, however, argue that although the conditions that allow for complex life are highly improbable, perhaps even unique, these conditions are still nothing more than an unintended fluke. The universe, after all, is a big place, with some 10^{22} stars in the part we can see. With so many opportunities, maybe at least one habitable planet will turn up just by chance. By itself, that seems to be a reasonable argument, especially if you don't consider any evidence for design from other scientific disciplines.

But what if we're not merely the winners of a blind cosmic lottery? What if our existence is the result of a conspiracy rather than a coincidence? Is there

---

[5] Ward and Brownlee (2000).

any way we could tell? Gonzalez and I argue that there is. It turns out that the same rare, finely tuned conditions that allow for intelligent life on Earth also make it strangely well suited for viewing, analyzing and discovering the universe around us.

The fact that we inhabit a terrestrial planet with a clear atmosphere and water on its surface; that our moon is just the right size and distance from Earth to stabilize the tilt of Earth's rotation axis; that our position in our large spiral galaxy is just so; that our sun is its precise mass and composition: all of these and many more are not only necessary for Earth's habitability; they also have been surprisingly crucial for scientists to discover the universe.

To put it more technically and more generally, "measurability" seems to correlate with habitability. Measurability refers to those features of the universe as a whole, and especially to our particular location in it—both in space and time—that allow us to detect, observe, discover, and determine the size, age, history, laws, and other properties of the physical universe. It's what makes scientific discovery possible.

Those rare pockets of habitability in our universe, as it happens, also allow for the most measurement. They're the best overall places for scientific discovery. This is strange because there's no obvious reason to assume that the very same rare properties that allow for observers would also provide the best overall setting for observing the world around them.

Of course, justifying such a claim requires a lot of evidence. But a couple of examples should be enough to illustrate what we mean by a "correlation between habitability and measurability."

A rare convergence of events allows Earthlings to witness not just solar eclipses, but *perfect* solar eclipses, where the Moon just barely covers the Sun's bright photosphere. Such eclipses depend on the precise sizes, shapes, and relative distances of the Sun, Moon, and Earth. There's no law of physics or celestial mechanics that requires the right configuration. In fact, of the more than 65 major moons in our Solar System, ours best matches the Sun as viewed from its planet's surface, and this is only possible during a fairly narrow window of Earth's history encompassing the present. The Moon is about 400 times smaller than the Sun. But right now, the Moon is about 400 times closer to the Earth than is the Sun. So, the Moon's apparent size on the sky matches the Sun's. Astronomers have noted this odd coincidence for centuries. And, since the Sun appears larger from the Earth than from any other planet with a moon, an Earth-bound observer can discern finer details in the Sun's chromosphere and corona than from any other planet. This makes our solar eclipses more valuable scientifically.

The recent pictures of solar eclipses sent back from the *Opportunity* rover on Mars nicely illustrate how much better our solar eclipses are. The two small potato-shaped Martian moons, Deimos and Phobos, appear much too small to cover the Sun's disk, and they zip across it in less than a minute.

It's intriguing that the best place to view total solar eclipses in our Solar System is the one time and place where there are observers to see them. It turns out that the precise configuration of Earth, Moon and Sun are also vital to sustaining life on Earth. A moon large enough to cover the Sun stabilizes the tilt of the rotation axis of its host planet, yielding a more stable climate, which is necessary for complex life. The Moon also contributes to Earth's ocean tides, which increase the vital mixing of nutrients from the land to the oceans. The two moons around Mars are much too small to stabilize its rotation axis.

In addition, it's only in the so-called Circumstellar Habitable Zone of our Sun—that cozy life friendly ring where water can stay liquid on a planet's surface—that the Sun appears to be about the same size as the Moon from Earth's surface. As a result, we enjoy perfect solar eclipses.

That alone seems fishy. But here's the part that suggests conspiracy rather than quirky coincidence. Our ability to observe perfect solar eclipses has figured prominently in several important scientific discoveries, discoveries that would have been difficult if not impossible on the much more common planets that don't enjoy such eclipses.

First, these observations helped disclose the nature of stars. Scientists since Isaac Newton (1666) had known that sunlight splits into all the colors of the rainbow when passed through a prism. But only in the 19th century did astronomers observe solar eclipses with spectroscopes, which use prisms. The combination of the man-made spectroscope with the natural experiment provided by eclipses gave astronomers the tools they needed not only to discover how the Sun's spectrum is produced, but the nature of the Sun itself. This knowledge enabled astronomers to interpret the spectra of the distant stars. So, in a sense, perfect eclipses were a key that unlocked the field of astrophysics.

Second, in 1919, perfect solar eclipses allowed two teams of astronomers, one led by Sir Arthur Eddington, to confirm a prediction of Einstein's General Theory of Relativity—that gravity bends light. They succeeded in measuring the changes in the positions of starlight passing near the Sun's edge compared to their positions months later. Such a test was most feasible during a perfect solar eclipse. The tests led to the general acceptance of Einstein's theory, which is the foundation of modern cosmology.

And finally, perfect eclipses give us unique access to ancient history. By consulting historical records of past solar eclipses, astronomers can calculate the change in Earth's rotation over the past several thousand years. This, in turn, allows us to put ancient calendars precisely on our modern calendar system.

These are just three ways in which perfect solar eclipses, produced by conditions that help create a habitable planet, have fostered scientific discovery. But this is only one example of the correlation between habitability and measurability.

At the much larger, galactic, scale, we again find that the most habitable place is also the best overall location for making a diverse range of scientific discoveries. Though the visible universe contains perhaps a hundred billion galaxies, astronomers group them into just three basic types: ellipticals, irregulars, and spirals. Our Milky Way is a spiral galaxy. Most of its stars are located in its flattened disk, its thickness is only about one percent its diameter. We live in the disk, very close to its midplane, about half way between the dangerous Galactic nucleus and its visible edge. Spiral galaxies like the Milky Way derive their popular name from the beautiful spiral pattern formed by their young stars and bright nebulae. We reside between the Sagittarius and Perseus spiral arms.

Contrary to popular impression, not all galaxies are equally habitable, since habitability depends on a galaxy's mass, type, age, and allotment of heavy elements. Moreover, even the relatively rare, large spiral galaxies like the Milky Way, which are likely optimal for life, probably contain only a few locations within a "Galactic Habitable Zone" compatible with complex life. Galaxies are filled with dangerous radiation hazards, and many regions are either so low in heavy elements as to prohibit terrestrial planets from forming, or so high that planetary systems will be hostile to life.

This Zone is an exclusive piece of real estate. In contrast, the inner ghetto of the Milky Way suffers from greater radiation threats and comet collisions, and an Earth-size planet is less apt to form there in a stable circular orbit. The outer regions are safer, but stars there will be accompanied by only fairly small terrestrial planets, planets too small to retain an atmosphere or sustain plate tectonics.

And the spiral arms are much more hostile to planetary systems aspiring to habitability than is our location between spiral arms. While we can't yet say how wide it is, the Galactic Habitable Zone seems to be a fuzzy ring in the thin disk at roughly the Sun's location, a ring whose habitability is itself compromised at several points where it intersects the spiral arms. If habitability depends on proximity to the so-called corotation circle--that region in which stars orbit at about the same speed as the spiral arm--then this thin and often broken ring could be narrower still.

At the same time, our location within the Galactic Habitable Zone offers the best overall location to be a successful astronomer and cosmologist. Even though we're near the mid-plane, there's very little in the way of dust in our neighborhood to absorb light from nearby stars and distant galaxies. We're far enough from the Galactic center and the disk is flat enough that it doesn't excessively obscure our view of the distant universe. We have access to a striking diversity of nearby stars and other Galactic structures, as well as a clear view of distant galaxies and the unique cosmic microwave background radiation, both essential for discovering the astonishing facts that the universe is expanding and finite in age.

These examples are merely illustrative. To be persuasive, the argument needs more detail, more evidence, and more rigor. Properly framed and developed, however, we think the evidence for the correlation between life and discovery forms a pervasive and telling pattern, a pattern that not only contradicts the Copernican Principle, but also suggests that the universe, whatever else it is, is designed for discovery.

Design? Surely no question in science is more interesting and more controversial. But it's surely a possibility, even if we've been discouraged from asking the question, let alone being encouraged to seek evidence for such a possibility. But in science, as in life, things can change. Perennial questions, even when officially ignored, have a way of bubbling up. Here, as elsewhere, we discern the activities of intelligent agency by certain types of patterns. And such patterns show up not just in the physical sciences, but in biology as well.

2.7 ID in Biology

Even once you have an environment suitable for life, you don't get life automatically. There remains the niggling problem of the origin of biological information. For instance, most of us have heard of the presence of information encoded along the DNA molecule. To many, it looks suspiciously like an extraordinarily sophisticated computer code for producing proteins, the three-dimensional building blocks of all life. And with the right cellular hardware, the code does just that.

But this isn't merely an impression of design. As early as 1968 chemist and philosopher Michael Polanyi saw that the information in that code stubbornly transcends its chemical medium, just as the letters and sentences of a book transcend the chemistry of ink and paper.[6] The attempt to reduce life to the

---

[6] See Polanyi (1968) and Polanyi (1967).

laws and physics and chemistry was doomed.

In the mid-1980's, Walter Bradley, Charles Thaxton and Roger Olsen dared to suggest in *The Mystery of Life's Origins*[7] that this was best explained by intelligent design. And in recent years, ID theorist Stephen Meyer has turned this evidence into a formidable argument for intelligent design. Meyer argues that the usual aimless processes of chance and chemistry can't explain this information.[8] Moreover, in our everyday experience, we know perfectly well where information of this sort comes from: intelligent agents.

Moving up a level, we find complex and functionally integrated machines that look out of reach to the Darwinian mechanism. Michael Behe immortalized some of these in his bestselling 1996 book, *Darwin's Black Box*.[9] If any evidence for intelligent design is mentioned in media reports, it's usually Behe's. Behe argues that these tiny molecular machines, such as the bacterial flagellum, are "irreducibly complex." They're like a mousetrap. Without all of their basic parts, they don't work. Natural selection can only build systems one small step at a time, by traversing a path in which each step provides a present survival advantage for the organism. It can't select for a future function. To do that requires foresight—the exclusive jurisdiction of intelligent agents. Such structures look very much like the systems produced by intelligent agents, who can foresee a future function and actualize it.

Notice that Behe's argument, like most good design arguments, is both negative *and* positive. On the one hand, he argues that the Darwinian mechanism is a bad explanation for these systems. On the other, he argues that they have just the features we normally attribute to intelligent agency. If you get this point, you've gotten beyond the apparent comprehension of most published criticisms of intelligent design.

Moving to the macroscopic world, there is the three dimensional complexity of many diverse animal body plans. In the fossil record, these show up at more or less the same time, geologically speaking. The point is not that there are "gaps in the fossil record." Of course there are, because not every moment of life's history is preserved in a deposit. The problem is the sudden appearance of complexity is not what the Darwinian story of gradual evolution would lead you to expect. In our experience, sudden innovations and massive infusions of information come from intelligent agents.

Finally, there are human agents themselves, which are so unexpected in materialist terms, that many materialists actually try to deny their existence.

---

[7] Thaxton et al. (1984).
[8] See, for instance, Meyer (2004).
[9] Behe (1996).

You see, the materialist rule about what science may consider, if followed consistently, leads consistent materialists to deny the existence of agents in general. That means you and I don't exist. As a general rule, any idea that entails that you don't exist is not an idea you should take seriously.

At the beginning of the 21st century, we look out at an utterly different world from that envisioned by the materialistic science of the late nineteenth century. But the materialistic definition of science inherited from the nineteenth century still prevents many from considering this new evidence.

This strange situation led Phillip Johnson in the 1990's, the grandfather of the intelligent design movement, to ask a singularly subversive question: If the materialistic definition of science and the scientific evidence are in conflict, should we go with the definition or the evidence?

To ask the question, as they say, is to answer it. *Scientia* means knowledge. Natural science is or should be the search for knowledge of the natural world. If we are properly scientific, then, we will seek to be open to the natural world, not decide beforehand what it's allowed to reveal.

This isn't rocket science. Either the universe provides evidence for purpose and design or it doesn't. Many argue that it doesn't. Even more argue that we're not allowed to ask the question, let alone seek an answer. They insist on "methodological naturalism," which is that the idea that scientists *qua* scientists must act as if materialism is true in their scientific work. But if the universe can provide evidence against design, then it could provide evidence for design. By force of logic, you can't have it both ways. Imposing an artificial definition of science is simply a way to avoid the dilemma rather than resolving it.

2.8   Saint Darwin

It's a strange feature of our current intellectual climate that one can almost safely raise the subject of design in physics and astronomy, but still not suggest that Darwin's theory of evolution might not be whole story in biology. In the wrong company, expressing doubts about Darwinism, quite apart from the question of intelligent design, is still the surest way for an intellectual, especially a scientist, to ruin a career or a cocktail party. I don't know why this is. Maybe it results from a dim awareness that Darwinism is the best story anyone has come up with for explaining away the appearance of design in biology, and no one is likely to think of a better replacement. In any case, it's clear that the devout Darwinists have decided to dig trenches where they are, rather than to retreat to more defensible terrain.

So be it. At some point its partisans will have to account for the failures of this creaky, nineteenth century conjecture. The Darwinian toolkit—natural selection and random variations—is quite limited. It's great for explaining trivial things that aren't much in dispute, and notorious for becoming narrative when it comes to explaining the really big stuff.[10] If you ask why finch beaks adapt to changing climate in the Galapagos Island, natural selection is quite the charmer. If you ask, however, for evidence for the Darwinian origin of the bacterial flagellum or the light sensitive spot, be prepared for a speculative yarn strung around precious little data. And if you're lucky, maybe you'll be insulted for asking the question.

But more telling than a mere lack of evidence, I think, is that the theory has consistently relied for its props on a small stable of half truths and misrepresentations. Think of almost anything you can remember about evolution from your tenth grade biology class. Go ahead, think. Probably any piece of evidence you can remember will wither when exposed to the elements, which is usually just the relevant scientific literature.

Biologist Jonathan Wells made many of these so-called "icons of evolution" infamous in his book by the same name published in 2000. Anyone who has bothered to read *Icons of Evolution*[11] now knows that much of what we believed was evidence for Darwinian evolution was either misleading or false. Remember those diagrams of vertebrate embryos, showing how similar they are early on in their development? The image is supposed to illustrate the common ancestry of vertebrates. The various classes—human, fish, chickens—express their common ancestry early in development, and then diverge as they develop.

Darwin called this the "single strongest class of facts" in favor of his theory. Alas, there were some problems. The original drawings, by Darwin's disciple Ernst Haeckel in the 19th century, were fudged. Haeckel cherry-picked the examples that looked the most alike. Then he made the least similar embryos look more alike than they really were. And then Haeckel started his drawings mid-way through development, where the animals happen to look most alike. The earliest stages in his diagram are not the earliest stages of development. Those stages, when many of the animals look strikingly different, are nowhere to be seen.

Then there are the famous peppered moths. You know the story. In England, the numbers of light and dark moths was known to fluctuate. The as-

---

[10] See the powerful argument for this point in Michael Behe's book, *The Edge of Evolution: The Search for the Limits of Darwinism* Behe (2007).

[11] Wells (2000).

sumption was that when industrial pollution darkened the lichen on the trunks of trees, this provided camouflage for the dark moths, which then began to predominate. When environmental regulations and better technology led to cleaner air, the tree trunks lightened again. The trunks then provided camouflage for the light moths, and they began to predominate. This was originally just a hunch, but then some famous field studies in the 1950s seemed to confirm that natural selection was indeed responsible. Birds were even witnessed eating the hapless moths, exposed as they were on the contrasting tree trunks. Natural selection in action! To quote George Tenet, the former director of the CIA, it was a slam dunk.

Now, even if this story had turned out alright, it wouldn't have shown much. The story is intuitively plausible. There are no random mutations to speak of. No story about where moths came from. There's just a diverse population of moths, waxing and waning as one group, and then the other, has a selective advantage. So it was doubly astonishing when this story started to unravel. In the 1980s, scientists began to realize that the proportions of light and dark moths had fluctuated in other parts of the world where the industrial pollution wasn't a factor. More stunning, moths aren't so fond of tree trunks. They like to rest under the branches of trees, where the camouflage doesn't make much difference. They're also nocturnal—again making the camouflage trivial. And, surprisingly, they tend to get eaten, not by bird, but by bats. Those nice pictures we've all seen of the moths on tree trunks are due to creative license. They are dead or sleepy moths placed on the trunks for a photo op.

There are lots of other just so stories like this in the Darwinian lore. Of course, any theory can have a bad day. Maybe Darwinism could be given the benefit of the doubt, if it weren't for the rank fanaticism with which it's defended. I'd be the first to give the theory the benefit of the doubt if it weren't for the perverse conduct of so many Darwinists. It just smells fishy. For example, for his efforts on behalf of scientific truth, Jonathan Wells has been accused of faking his credentials (false), of never having done scientific research (false), and especially vilified for his presumed religious beliefs, such as his affiliation with the Unification Church. But calling Jonathan Wells a Moonie is not going to put those moths back on the tree trunks.

2.9 Starting to Stick

Critics of intelligent design frequently report on the imminent demise of intelligent design, even as they give it another kick, just in case. But there is no evidence that the issue will disappear anytime soon. In fact, despite the controversy and hatred it engenders in some quarters, the arguments of contemporary design theorists are having an effect. Consider the case of Antony Flew. For over fifty years, the British philosopher has been the English-speaking world's most intellectually serious public atheist. He first debated C.S. Lewis at Oxford in 1950, and has pursued scholarly defenses of atheism until recently. He has always argued that there just wasn't enough evidence to believe in God. In December, at age 81, he told the world that he had changed his mind.

So what did it for Flew? It wasn't a religious conversion. In an interview with philosopher Gary Habermas he attributes his new view not to any religious text but to *scientific* evidence, in particular, evidence of intelligent design: ". . . I think the argument to Intelligent Design is enormously stronger than it was when I first met it."[12] In an interview with the *Associated Press* (Dec. 9, 2004), Flew said "his ideas have some similarity with American 'intelligent design' theorists."

When Flew says he believes in "God," he doesn't mean he's put his trust in the God of Bible. He's referring to the generic "God of the Philosophers"—a First Cause, postulated on the basis of evidence and rational argument. He understands as well as anyone that design arguments don't prove the existence of God in all the fullness of religious belief. At best, they point the mind in that direction. And it's that *implication*, obviously, that is creating widespread metaphysical panic among our academic and cultural elites.

In an ideal world, these issues would be debated rationally, the evidence evaluated dispassionately rather than ruled out of bounds by definition, and conclusions reached without regard to the implications. But not this evidence, and not with these implications. Certain ideas in science have and will always have theological implications, for good or ill. As arch-Darwinist Richard Dawkins so memorably said: "Darwin made it possible to be an intellectually fulfilled atheist." OK, so what happens if Darwinism goes the way of Marxism and phrenology? And what happens if the word gets out that evidence from science points in a direction that Richard Dawkins would prefer not to go?

Everyone knows that a universe that looks designed for a purpose encourages all sorts of interesting theological questions. Lots of intellectuals don't want to go there. So we should not be surprised that they are reacting with equal parts fury and indignation at all this talk about intelligent design. In our current climate, even the bare rumor of God causes some among us to reach for the long knives and start stabbing.

I predict that this strategy will fail. Antony Flew's change of mind is a snapshot of the changing state of a debate many hoped was settled once and

---

[12] Flew and Habermas (2005). Find it at http://www.biola.edu/antonyflew/.

for all in the nineteenth century. The genie is out of the bottle. The mandarins can no longer control the flow of information to those who thirst for it. Ad hominem arguments and indignant and uninformed bloviations will not put this genie back in the bottle. Any effective argument against intelligent design will have to target real intelligent design arguments like the ones described here, not the caricatures preferred by hostile critics.

Jay W. Richards, Ph.D., is Research Fellow and Director of Acton Media at the Acton Institute in Grand Rapids, Michigan. He is the co-author with astronomer Guillermo Gonzalez of *The Privileged Planet: How Our Place in the Cosmos is Designed for Discovery* (Regnery, 2004).

Chapter 3

Evolution or Intelligent Design

Lennart Nørreklit
Department for Education, Learning and Philosophy
Aalborg University
Denmark

Summary

1. The problem is delimited to the rationality of the argument from intelligent design, AID. Then a number of elements involved in the argument are described, and for each of them, problems of rationality are demonstrated:

2. The inference from design to a designer is analyzed and not seen as rationally sound in AID.

3. The identification of intelligence is analyzed — AID breaks down our paradigm of intelligence.

4. The content of intelligence and intelligent structure is illuminated. AID appears incompatible with the content of the concept of intelligence.

5. The notion of a purpose appears necessary and is analyzed. The concept of purpose has no transcendent use as in AID.

6. The romantic notion of creationism is contrasted with the notion of evolution. Evolution explains the development of intelligence.

7. The argument from unique values of the natural constants of the universe is analyzed. This supports the idea of evolution, which somehow contradicts AID.

8. Summary of the reflection of human concepts as immanent in nature.

9. Some of the main points are illustrated with excerpts from one of the oldest philosophical texts on creation, the Brhadaranyaka Upanishad and more.

3.1 The Question: The Rationality of the Argument

The argument from intelligent design claims to be based on scientific evidence. It observes phenomena in the world that seem to be highly intelligently designed while at the same time one can see no way of explaining their existence by means of natural causes. In the beginning it was the information complexity of the DNA molecule that stunned the scholars. Recently it was the astonishing fine-tuning of the natural constants of the universe needed to make life as we know it possible. Also the discovery of amazing and apparently unexplainable nanotechnological 'engines' around us called for a special explanation. With this lack of explanation the adherents of intelligent design found a solution: There is an intelligent designer who designed these amazing phenomena.

Our question is: Is this way of explaining things really a way of explaining anything? Say we discover a phenomenon, and we do not know how it is produced. To calm our puzzled state of mind and to answer our questions, we introduce the idea of a creator of this inexplicable phenomenon. We do not know anything about this producer, except that he produces what we cannot understand. — In former times, when, say, a disease hit people, some of them thought that there was a producer of the plague that punished them for something. So they asked for forgiveness to God, hoping he would forgive them their sins and heal them. Or if a catastrophic event happened, such as the eruption of a volcano, this could be explained by a god who produced volcanoes and set them on fire to punish people if he got mad at them. Unexplainable phenomena have always existed. Before the emergence of science, many of these phenomena were explained as the will of some God that therefore was introduced. That the appearance of very complex and apparently purposeful

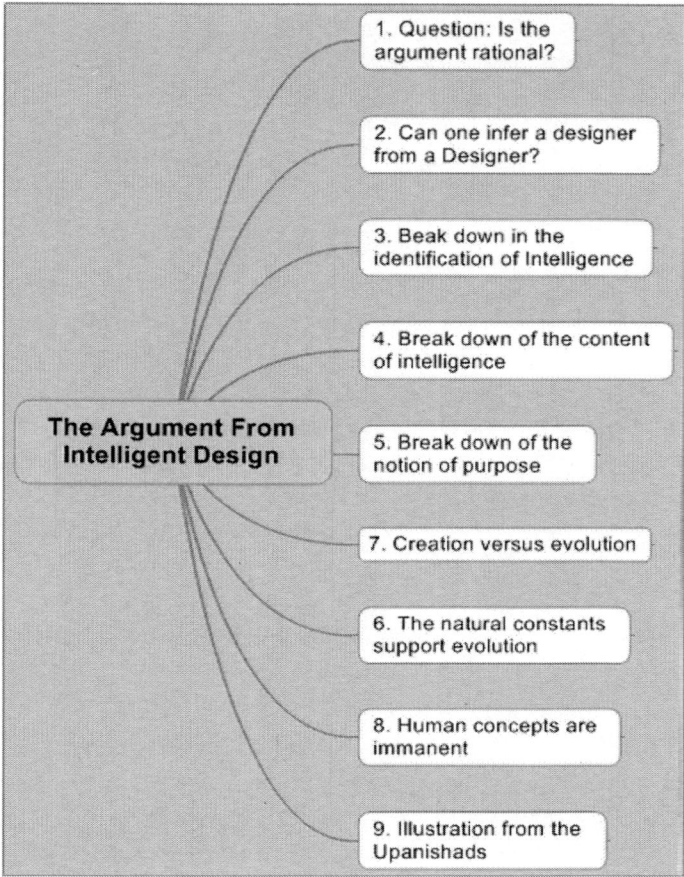

Figure 3.1: Outline

phenomena in nature could trigger the same form of shortcut explanations is hardly surprising. But do we really get any explanation? Have we become any wiser as to how the DNA molecule was constructed, how the constants of the universe were determined or how the nanomachines were constructed by introducing a designing God? Not a bit. It appears clearly superstitious. Why then do some people consider this line of though an explanation at all?

There was a time at which philosophers and theologians debated whether God's existence could be *proved*. A number of so called proofs of the existence of God were constructed such as the cosmological, the teleological and the ontological proofs of God's existence. These so called proofs have been subject to analysis and criticism for centuries. The status of this analysis is that there are no valid proofs of the existence of God. In general it seems reasonable to follow a Kantian criticism, that our concepts have validity in the empirical world only. Any attempt to jump from a worldly use of our concepts to a transcendent use is unfounded and violates the condition for rational use of our concepts.

In recent times an apparently new argument — the argument from intelligent design — has been added to the list of arguments. It is clearly familiar with some of the old well known arguments, but its followers claim that it is special in the way it uses modern scientific insight in the construction of the universe and the complexities of life as its evidence. Also they claim that the evidence is not the evidence for God as a creator but as a designer. According to the argument, the world is incomprehensibly complex and looks as if designed in such an advanced way, that the most amazing systems are possible, such as the nanomachines, DNA, life, and higher forms of intelligence. This design is so unlikely, so special, unique and intelligent, that it — according the adherents — seems reasonable to conclude, that there must be a special and incredibly intelligent designer, who created or shaped the world in precisely this manner.

However, one question is whether God's existence as designer can be *proved*. A different question is whether we nevertheless have *arguments* for or against the existence of a creating and shaping God. Although an argument is not a proof, this does not necessarily mean that it is a bad argument. We use arguments all the time and with great success that are in no way proofs. Instead of arguing that something *proves* something else, one may more cautiously and more realistically talk about that something *points in the direction of* something or that something makes something more *likely*, or that it *indicates* or is a *symptom* of something. One may consider something as *evidence* for something else and use it in one's arguments. The question is: Is there and can there be any evidence in the world that points towards something outside the world. How can anything in the world point towards something outside the world?

Evidence can be more or less strong and convincing. In order for an argument to be a good argument, the evidence must be strong and maybe not absolute but nevertheless rather convincing. This means that there must be a basis for judging the strength of the evidence. This basis is normally of a comparative nature. One may for instance have the *experience* that if A occurs then B also occurs. Thus, based on experience, one compares a number of cases. If experience shows that every time A occurs, then B also occurs, then A may be considered to be evidence for B. How good this evidence is depends on the extension and quality of the experience upon which it is based.

When a person claims the existence of a phenomenon, B, and argues for this claim by reference to the existence of an other phenomenon, A, then this is a good argument, if the relation between the existence of A and the existence of B is documented in experience or through systematic scientific studies — that is, if A is good evidence for B.

Thus the following questions arise: How can any experience — which is in all respects according to its very meaning, is something in the world - point at something outside the world? And: How can any experience point towards something of which we know nothing?

These criteria for good evidence and good argument illustrate that arguments in favor of the existence of the designer or creator God cannot be good arguments. When claiming the existence of God the designer then there is not and cannot be any comparative basis, which can be used to justify whether the evidence is good or not. It is impossible to have a comprehensive *experience* of or *scientific study* about the relation between God and the world - unless God is redefined as a phenomenon that is to be found in the empirical world. But precisely this is logically impossible for God as the creator of the world.

It may be objected that it is not the creator God but the designer God that is concerned. However, either the influence of the act of designing was finished with creation, with the beginning of the world. If this is the case, then the objection applies; evidence of God's presence cannot be found in the world because that would mess up his design. Or the design continued as a guiding principle for God to intervene as the universe develops. This would however imply an intervening unpredictable God who needs to adjust his design as it goes along. This would amongst other things contradict the claim of a general scientific attitude.

Despite the difference between the ideas of God as the creator of the world and God as the designer of the world or some phenomena in the world, God is in both cases considered as the creator: In the one case as creator of the world. In the other case he is considered the creator of the intelligent design of the world. Even within the believers in the argument from intelligent design the element of creation is important: God did not only design the natural constants so that the universe can support life, the made them obtain this value — he created or ensured the reality of the design. The points about the nanomachines especially underline this point. They are not only very smart — i.e. they embody an intelligent design. But apparently, the argument runs, they cannot be naturally constructed — i.e. they have to be created in a supernatural way, by God who therefore is not only designer but also creator. The same applies to the argument concerning the DNA.

Even if one cannot claim that some arguments are more or less *good*, it may still be possible to talk about whether there *are* arguments for the existence of God and that God created the world. The statement, that God created the world, is not irrational as long as one can claim that there are *arguments* — rational arguments — for the existence of God the creator. Only if there are no such arguments, or if the arguments or the statement itself involves contradictions or absurdities, then there is no rational basis for the belief in God as the creator.

The subject of the analysis that follows is concerned with clarifying the nature and rationality of the argument from intelligent design by studying various aspects involved in it. Our question is whether the argument is a clear, rational argument or not.

3.2 The Inference from Design to a Designer

The inference from something that *appears* as an intelligent design to the existence of an intelligent designer is very common and normally unproblematic and trivial. It is usually based on extensive human experience. Almost all human products and constructs embody an intelligent design. We know that this design does not come by itself. It presupposes an active designer who made the design as well as the producers who managed to implement the design in an intelligent product. The question is whether there is something special about the intelligent design that enables us to recognize it as such?

Normally our understanding of the design of a product is sufficient to enable us to distinguish when we are confronted with a product embodying intelligent design and when not. Things with intelligent design are produced by intelligent designers, and of these we only know human beings. We know from the human world what a (human) intelligent design is, and we know how such designed products differ from things that are not so designed but simply phenomena of nature.

After having investigated a drawing the connoisseur art specialist concludes for instance: "This is a genuine Picasso!" He recognizes that this drawing is highly intelligent — only a great artist could produce it. And based on style and many other details he concludes that it must be Picasso who made the drawing. Thus he makes an inference from the design to the designer. He could be mistaken — it might be a fake drawing, an imitation of Picasso. But even an imitation of Picasso presupposes a Picasso to imitate — the designer, Picasso must exist or have existed. This line of reasoning works, because Picasso is a well known painter. However, suppose that that the specialist had concluded: "This is a genuine Godasso!" However, nobody *knows* anything about the painter named Godasso. What would this mean? When confronted with the question: "Who is Godasso?" he answers: "Godasso is 'the Great Painter' — the super painter who inspired all other painters and made countless of secret paintings that cannot be ascribed to any immanent painter." This clearly transcends the rational study of painting and moves the discourse into a world of belief with no rational foundation as far as paintings are concerned.

In the history of philosophy one may compare the argument from intelligent design with Descartes's inference from the "I think" to the existence of a thinking substance, i.e. a substance that creates the thinking. Kant points out that this inference is not valid. Similarly the inference from a 'design' of the world or something in the world to a divine substance that envisioned that design is not valid. Although there is evidence that *could* point to an intelligent design, one cannot on this basis conclude, that there is an intelligent designer. The argument is not even a good argument for the existence of a Divine designer because we never experience anything linking God and the design together. That is pure speculation.

Occasionally, people encounter problems or puzzles involved in this inference to a designer. For instance: A white figure on a plaza in Berlin looks like a sculpture of a human being — that is: an intelligent design. After some hours it reveals itself as a human being — not a sculpture. The artist himself stood as a piece of art. He made himself to an embodied design for a couple of hours. Now this is an exception. That is why it creates attention. People wonder: How could he control his breathing and movement so much? But the case just underlines the need for a comparative basis of experience, which enables us to judge, whether there in the specific case is any reason to assume the existence of an independently existing designer.

Everyday experience on the other hand demonstrates an abundance of examples of the creation of something extremely complex and intelligently constructed that definitively has not been designed by any designer. That is the secret of living things. Living things are created by other living things without any designer intervening. Parents may want to get children. The design of the child happens when the sperm fertilizes the egg. It is in this process that the genes which embody the design of the coming being are finally selected. No designer was involved. The parents did not design the child — they had no idea of its specific properties before they discovered them by experience. It is obvious that the most complicated phenomena we know — the human brain — are designed in a process where no designer operates. Then why should we

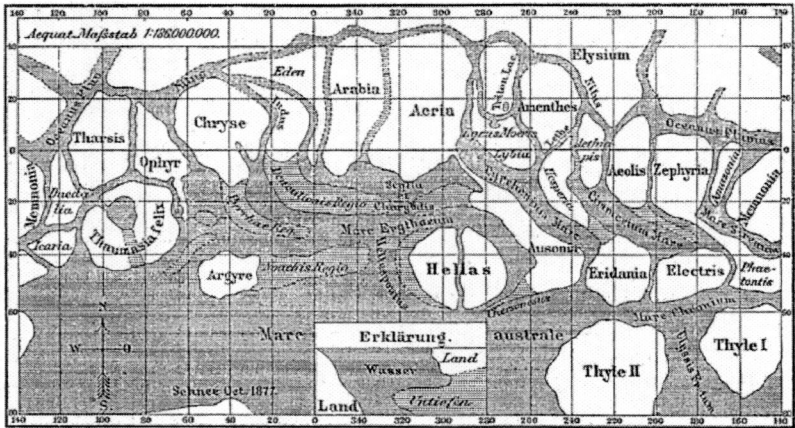

Figure 3.2: Schiaparelli's map of Mars.

believe that it is necessary to assume the working of an unknown designer in other complicated cases of Mother Nature?

The argument from design specifically relates to scientific evidence and scientific experience. It is not the first time that the wonders of the world have led scientists to believe in intelligent design. For instance, in 1877 the Italian astronomer Giovanni Schiaparelli observed distinct straight lines on the planet Mars. These lines gave the clear impression of being created by some kind of intelligence — they were not natural. They were interpreted as canals. Here was — it appeared — the first observation of an intelligent design that had no human origin. The conclusion seemed obvious: There had to be some intelligent designers. They were not human beings. They had to be inhabitants on Mars. The Marsians were finally detected (see Figure 3.2[1]).

In the nineteenth century it was not uncommon to assume that all the planets were inhabited. The general concept of evolution had entered the scientific scene during the late eighteenth century. It led to the imagination that evolution of civilizations evolved on the planets, as it had happened on Earth. For instance, the great natural scientist H. C. Ørsted (1777-1851), the discoverer of electromagnetism, who was inspired by the philosopher Immanuel Kant, believed that all planets were inhabited. Such imagination probably influenced some astronomers, and when Schiaparelli finally eyed the lines on Mars, many saw this as a sensational discovery of an intelligent design created by an alien

---

[1] Image from WikiMedia Commons:
http://en.wikipedia.org/wiki/Image:Karte_Mars_Schiaparelli_MKL1888.png

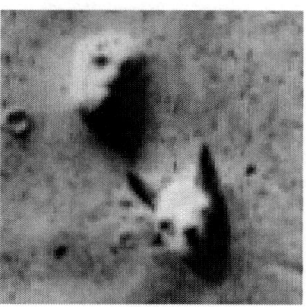

Figure 3.3: Human and animal face on Mars (Photo from NASA).

civilization. The sensational news made many astronomers take a sharper look at Mars and some of them were able as Schiaparelli to see the canals — or what ever it was — on Mars. In 1910, Percival Lowell even wrote a book, *Mars As the Abode of Life*, in which he described Mars as a dying planet on which the inhabitants had constructed an enormous irrigation system to distribute water from polar regions to the population centers near the equator.

However, astronomers soon realized that the so called canals in reality are optical illusions. Today such illusions can easily be replicated. The observed "canals" were the result of an intelligent design, namely the design of our perception. Schiaparelli had observed the effect of our own design and not that of any Marsians.

Still today, Mars is the subject of romantic imaginations. There is for instance a special formation on Mars, which looks like a human face. This has also inspired romantic visions about some special spiritual messages of some kind, although in reality the formation is just a natural formation in Mars' landscape.

The search for life on Mars still goes on, but now on a more scientifically sound basis. It is however, not long ago, that some scientist thought they had made the sensational discovery of traces of life on Mars based on a number of photos and evidence from a meteorite from Mars. Also, they argued that the evidence could only be produced through living organism and not by a lifeless nature.[2] But later they had to admit that their findings were inconclusive.

The same form of romantic argumentation is sometimes given by modern adventurers when they during their underwater search for the fabled sunken Atlantis stumble across deep underwater formations which to them look like

---

[2] See the story at http://seds.org/spaceviews/hotnews/mars-story.html

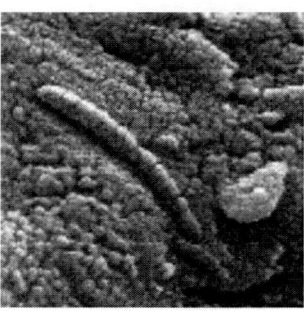

Figure 3.4: A trace of previous life on Mars?

expressions of intelligent design. Sometimes they are convinced that the formations are intelligently designed although according to scientists it is most likely natural phenomena created by nature.

All such arguments seem to express a wishful thinking. We may as human beings have a natural tendency to think this way. To *believe* in it is, however, superstition and not a rational attempt to explain and understand. We posses no evidence of God himself and we therefore cannot by experience establish evidence of any other phenomenon as connected to God. There is nothing in our evidence that points outside the universe — the reference from the observed to God the designer and creator is in the mind only.

3.3 The identification of intelligence

Human products are the realization of an intelligent design — at least some of them, others are badly designed. What makes a design look intelligent, how is it identified? It is normally not difficult to identify things that are designed intelligently. Say, a car: A car embodies a very intelligent, a very clever design. And it is easily identified as an intelligent design. It is clearly something different from natural phenomena such as rocks, raindrops, waves etc. that — apparently — cannot be characterized as the embodiment of any intelligent design. We do not even need to drive it in order to see that it is an intelligent design. We know just by looking at it. It looks designed by an intelligent being. The design of the car has developed and become more and more intelligent. Intelligence is always a question of degree, and there are different types of intelligence.

The different between nature and the intelligent design is not, that nature is chaotic and lacks structure and form. It has a lot of structure and complex forms. If that was not the case, then nobody could live in it. However, although it has a lot of structure, this normally does not make us hesitate in our judgment as to what things embody an intelligent design and what things do not. Although errors occasionally occur, one can normally easily distinguish between objects that embody human intelligent design, and natural objects, that do not. This is possible for us, because we as human beings know what human beings are creating and how this normally differs in appearance from the phenomena of nature.

Thus observation of the presence of intelligent design is at least partly based on knowledge of the nature of the form-world of the intelligent designer and how this form-world differs from the form-world of nature. Whether it be a modern product with advanced technology — such as a car or a personal computer — or whether it is old technology — for instance a stone ax — is irrelevant. So far, in every case the form-world of the intelligent design clearly differs from the form-world of nature. Nature is in all cases contrasted with the form world of the intelligent design. However, with the modern technology of genetic engineering this difference seems to become smaller and smaller, and we may soon be confronted with products where we are unable to decide, whether they are natural or contain elements of intelligent design.

The idea of an argument from intelligent design presupposes a distinction between that which is intelligently designed and that which is not. If this distinction cannot be upheld, then the very meaning of the notion of intelligent design as pointing to a designer dissolves.

However, if the world itself as a whole is created by an intelligent designer then there is no such distinction. Then one must presume that also the stone, the grain of sand and all other natural phenomena embody intelligent design — even a design that is much more intelligent than the design *we* use to create cars and computers. Thus, if the *world* is made according to an intelligent design, then what we used to call intelligent design, i.e. human artefacts, are the opposite, namely rather unintelligent design compared to the advanced design of, say, stones and other natural phenomena.

Thus by extending the concept of intelligent design to encompass the design of the whole universe and thus of all nature, the very distinction between that which is intelligent design and that which is not intelligent design breaks down. It even creates the conclusion, that that which by paradigmatic definition is defined as intelligent design, human artefacts, in reality — whatever that might mean here — is a rather unintelligent design at least as far as the human component of these products is concerned. It is difficult to see how a concept can rationally survive being in conflict with its own paradigmatic definition.

The conceptual mess which the argument from intelligent design thus forces upon us, does not destroy the argument as argument, but it contradicts the rationality of the argument. The imagination, that something that we know from ourselves and our fellow human beings as intelligent can be attributed to a transcendent absolute being approaches the absurd. What can "absolute intelligence" possibly mean? And if God has no absolute intelligence, then we are stuck in a ridiculous anthropomorphism.

Statements such as "The nanomachine" (for instance) "looks smart/intelligent" and "We cannot explain how the nanomachine is created" may be seen as pointing towards a non-natural explanation. However, they do not express any form of evidence. While statements such as "The nanomachine is a complex system" and "The nanomachine does so and so" may express evidence, they do however not point towards any form of explanation.

3.4 Intelligence and design models

To design something is to make a model of it. However, one may sometimes consider design and model as two opposite perspective. The design may be seen as a priori because it normally comes before the phenomenon of which it is a design. The design therefore may be used prescriptively. The model on the other hand may sometimes be seen as a model of something that already exists in which case it is something a posteriori.

An intelligent being is able to reflect all kinds of things in its environment because it is able to construct models for all kinds of things. Every flexible medium potentially contains the design of any other thing.

This ability to reflect the structure of other things plays a distinct role in the history of philosophy. Plato's use of the metaphor of the wax block on which memory inscribes our ideas is an early illustration of this ability.[3]

An interesting case is found in Leibniz' philosophy. He considered all things — monads — as a mirror of the whole universe. The universe is mirrored in every substance according to him. Every substance contained in itself the model (design) of the whole universe. This established what he considered the universal harmony. This universe is on the other hand one great calculus, one system that covers the whole space-time universe. This appears incompatible with the modern view of the universe, where different systems compete to survive. Another problem we have with Leibniz' philosophy is that the mirroring is not a genuine model because it has an infinite complexity. Leibniz'

---

[3] Plato: *Theaetetus*.

reflecting model is not a model in our sense, because it reflects everything like a mirror or a photo. A design or a model is as an abstraction that focuses on certain elements that makes up an important structure of what it reflects.

A more recent philosophy in this line is Wittgenstein's *Tractatus*.[4] In *Tractatus* the ability of one thing — a medium — to mirror the (logical) structure of other phenomena is central. For instance: The structure of the music is mirrored in the score notes as well as in the records, or the structure of the sound is mirrored in the structure of the electromagnetic impulses sent through the telephone line, and especially the structure of everything can be reflected in language. In modern technology the computer is the favored instrument to mirror everything. The construction of a model in *Tractatus* appears to be flexible as to the question of abstraction. One may create genuine models; it appears, as the engineer's design of a product. But Wittgenstein also seems to accept structural replica that are infinite in detail, as the analogue engravings in an old-fashioned record. The acceptance of the analogue mirroring as a way of generating structural resemblance appears however not fully consistent with the dominating digital perspective of the book.

Still today we have a certain tension between an analogue and a digital perspective. The analogue technique based on classical physics and the corresponding technology is increasingly replaced by digital technology of the IT-age. Precisely the IT-technology may be seen as a realization of the analysis of language described in *Tractatus*. Wittgenstein's vision of analyzing language into elementary digitally constructed propositions that precisely represents the meaning is very much what is done in modern programming. The ability to project a structure into a model which again can be projected into another model is infinite, it appears.

The ability to reflect a model is in itself a dead form of intelligence. It can be done by ink on a piece of paper or by a computer. It can reflect but not create. Such intelligence can carry a model of the structure of other things. But a living intelligence can do more than that. It can create and *transform* the models in its own way and thereby develop prescriptive designs for all kinds of things for all kinds of purposes. This complex ability is characteristic of the intelligence of advanced living beings. In it we see the idea of *Tractatus*, of the ability to mirror the structure of the world but we also see a reason why this must be supplemented with a quite different set of ideas on how to abstract, transform and act as in Wittgenstein's later philosophy.

Thus we characterize intelligence as the ability to reflect the world and design new solutions to the problems of life based on this reflection. It enables

---

[4] Wittgenstein (1922).

the intelligent being to achieve control over their environment — not by being stronger than the environment but by being smarter, more intelligent. It develops new solutions based upon the models that reflect the world.

This means, that an intelligent being that exists without any such systemic complexity which allows it to mirror something is incomprehensible because it is not intelligent. We have a lot of knowledge about how this is done for instance in the studies of language and consciousness. Psychology has even developed various intelligence tests.

What we cannot do is to understand intelligence — what intelligence is — if we place it outside the world. Our very concept of intelligence presupposes that the intelligent being is within in a world. Otherwise there would be nothing to model and no problems to solve.

The argument from intelligent design however violates this condition. It attributes intelligence to an imagined being that is outside the world. As a designer of the world, God must exist outside and before it. By applying the concept of intelligence to something outside the world, it loses its meaning. — We cannot, for instance, imagine an intelligence test for something outside the world, and we can definitely not do so for an absolute being.

3.5 The Role of Purpose

An intelligent design presupposes a purpose. The intelligence of the design largely depends on how smart it is to fulfill its purpose. The intelligence of the design of for instance a car depends partly on how well it solves its purpose of providing transportation. In order for the argument from intelligent design to function, it must be possible to use the concept of purpose in a meaningfully in the argument.

The purpose of an artefact is especially important in archeological studies. It is a key to understanding the artefact and its role in the society, thereby contributing to uncovering the culture and life of that society. The artefacts are recognizable as such when they are found. They look as if they are produced by human beings. This tells the archaeologist that they are produced in an intelligent way and that they fulfilled a purpose. However, often the purpose of is not known. This may make the artefact appear mysterious and inspire to explanations that they are the result of the design and working of a higher intelligence.

A case in point is the 2000 year old Naza lines. Across about 500 square kilometers of the Peruvian pampas we find the huge images of trapezoids and imaginary animals drawn by long straight lines that are etched in the earth.

Figure 3.5: Huge figure drawn by Naza lines, Peru.

Some of the lines are 10 kilometers long, and the whole design can only be seen from the air. They clearly represent some form of intelligent design. But their purpose as well the question how they could be produced by an ancient human culture have been mysterious and led to fanciful ideas such as runways for alien spaceships, ancient minimalist art, and more. The wild guessing is the result of the unsolved riddles concerning how and why they were produced. Although these questions are still not definitively answered, there is no doubt that they were created by human beings and that there is no need to introduce super intelligent beings from an alien culture.

The inference from an artefact to its purpose presupposes knowledge of the nature and life conditions of the people who used and designed it. Artefacts are intelligent attempts to satisfy the wishes and needs of human beings.

If an artefact was produced by a different but unknown kind of intelligent beings of which we have no knowledge, then we cannot reconstruct and understand the design, because we cannot know its function. We can reconstruct the function of human artefacts du to our knowledge of the skills and needs of human beings. Percival Lowell imagined that he could explain the intelligent design of the canals on Mars because the imagined the Marsians as a civilization much like a human civilization on Earth: Water is needed to grow crops. So he thought he understood some of the living conditions on Mars and the needs of the Marsians and thus he determined the purpose of the canals. The very need of the canals demonstrated, that the Marsians had great problems.

Needs and purposes are understood as some kind of tension in the relation between the being and the world it is in. However, if one has no knowledge of a certain being, and if that being is outside the world, then one can attach no needs or any purpose to it.

An inference from an object to the existence of a designer of which one does not know anything and of which one cannot know anything thus appears incomprehensible because we cannot ascribe a purpose to this designer.

In order to understand the wishes and needs of a designer — if he exists — one must place him in a world. If he is placed in the world then we can begin to understand how the designed object may create a difference with respect to the satisfaction of wishes and needs. Thus intelligent design presupposes a purpose — a wish or a need.

The world itself has neither needs nor problems. But neither has anything before and independent of any world.

The idea of creation by intelligent design calls for unanswerable questions such as, what a creator might want to accomplish with this creation? What could his purpose be? Either he wants to accomplish something with it — and then he wants some form of interaction with it — or it is a form of entertainment to him. But in this case there is no reason for it to be real — it might equally well just be a dream.

3.6 Evolution versus Design

The central conflict is the difference between the approach of evolution and that of creation. After having worked with the concepts of intelligence, design and purpose we are now in a position to clarify the distinction between the perspectives of evolution and creation.

The distinction between creation and evolution is traditionally related to two other distinctions which, however, emerge as less clear and conclusive. First there is the distinction between idealism and materialism. Religion and creationism is traditionally considered as idealistic while evolution is considered to be materialistic and scientific. The distinction between idealism and materialism is less clear when we are concerned with creation of models, having purposes and creating intelligent designs.

Secondly there is the distinction between gradual changes and leaps or jumps in a process of development. Today, evolution includes gradual changes taking a long time as well as radical changes happening in a short period of time, for instance due to great natural events.

Hegel's philosophy of development is normally characterized as dialectical and idealistic. The most important thing about his philosophy from our perspective here is, however, that it is a philosophy of development in which *development is conceived as an intelligent process — it is conceived as a process of objectification of increasingly intelligent structures.*

Often Hegel's dialectics of development was popularized with model "thesis — anti-thesis and synthesis". The first step in the model — the move from thesis to anti-thesis — is often characterized as a quantitative step of gradual changes in one direction. While the second step that leads from the conflict between thesis and anti-thesis to the synthesis, is a qualitative leap. This is however not Hegel's formulation of his dialectics. Nor is it Hegelian because it does not reveal the essential feature just mentioned, that development is a process in which more and more intelligent structures are objectified.

Later, the concept of development found its scientific basis in Darwin's description of the process of natural evolution. According to this theory, evolution of the species is a gradual process, driven by an ongoing process of mutation combined with a natural selection ensures the survival of those with the fittest qualities. Development is thus driven by a continuous process of improvement in adaptation. The theory of evolution was considered as a materialistic explanation of the process of development.

What Darwin's explanation does not tell is what it is that makes a species more or less fit for survival. This is, however, understandable from a Hegelian point of view. The Hegelian concept that development moves from a lower degree of intelligence to a higher degree of intelligence fills that gap. Translated to Darwinian terms this means that the fittest being normally is the one that is the most intelligently designed. This follows from our description of intelligence as the ability to reflect one's environment. The relevance of the conflict between the Darwinian materialism and a Hegelian idealism seems to vanish with the concept of intelligent structures. The other difference, between the gradual development of evolution and the shift between gradual and radical development in Hegelian dialectics is also less significant.

The approach of evolution is the opposite of a creationist approach including the approach from intelligent design. Creation is a movement from high intelligence of a designer to the designed which has a lower level of intelligence. The designer cannot create a design more intelligent than he is. The creator has higher intelligence than that which he creates; the designer has a higher intelligence than the designed. A creationist perspective in this sense is found in for instance Plato's philosophy where the development in time is a development from the perfect to the imperfect. The origin is perfect — then things go downhill with the emergence of the empirical world. Similarly, the Romantic Movement that preceded Hegel's philosophy also looked back in time to a golden age and considered history as a process of decay. Thus creationism embeds a romantic and somewhat pessimistic structure in contrast to the theories of evolution.

The difference between an evolutionary perspective in a Hegelian sense on the one hand and a creationist perspective in a Platonic sense on the other is basic in Karl R. Popper's book, *The open society and its enemies*[5]. He rejects both perspectives because they are too a priori or metaphysical to his mind. He rejects the romantic creationist perspective, which he attributes to Plato, and he rejects the dialectical developmental approach of Hegel and Marx. These approaches exceed the limits of reasoning according to Popper. He believes that they create a closed dogmatism because they are not open to empirical confrontation and possible refutation. Popper distinguishes between the empirical scientific approach which he wants to save, and the holistic philosophical approach of Hegel and Plato, which he opposes. However, Popper overlooks the nature of the rational element in explanation. Darwin's principle "the survival of the fittest" is itself self-evident, it is logical and cannot therefore be empirically refuted — nevertheless it largely explains the empirical fact of evolution. Also, Hegel is by far not a metaphysical philosopher. His description of development of historical processes as for instance the history of philosophy or the development of the human mind can be confronted with experience. Furthermore, Popper himself uses a philosophy that is based on logical principles — his criticism of Plato, Marx and Hegel should therefore rebound on himself.

In *Objective knowledge*[6] Popper himself finally reaches a philosophy of development in which he transforms his principles of scientific development into a general structure for development along lines similar to the Hegel-Darwin synthesis indicated above. Here Popper describes a mechanism of development in which more intelligent structures emerge out of structures with less intelligence. Theories — whether they are expressed in language or embedded in genetic structures — serve to solve problems of life. Experience demonstrates the weak spots of the operating theories, their errors. Thus new problems are created and with it the need for improved, more intelligent theories. Such theories then emerge in a random process. Most of them will immediately be eliminated as unfit. The fit ones take over until new experiences demonstrate their weaknesses.

The structure of evolution:

$$\to P_1 \to H \to EE \to P_2 \to$$

The structure of evolution starts with a specific problem, P_1. This is solved by a hypothesis or theory, H. The theory may for instance be the genetic struc-

---

[5] Popper (1945).
[6] Popper (1972).

ture or any other operating model. Then there is a process of error elimination, *EE*. In this process, experience or practice finds the errors and weak spots of the hypothesis. This defines a new problem that then must be solved by another hypothesis.

Popper's theory of development is basically the same as the Darwinian mechanism of evolution. The creation of the hypothesis by a process is random — as is the mutation in Darwinism. And Popper's error elimination is very much the same as Darwin's natural selection. Popper's formulation has the advantage that is describes a development of more and more intelligent structures.[7]

Thus the nature of evolution is that something more intelligent emerges from something less intelligent.

When we look at the raw physical forces of nature, this may appear unlikely. It appears much easier to understand that these forces can destroy that which is intelligent through natural forces than to imagine that they can create intelligent structures. And destroying something reduces it to unintelligent waste. However, the constructive forces of nature also exist. They are somewhat slow, because life grows and unfolds in a slow process. However, we know that the most complicated life-forms procreate without the need of an intelligent designer. It is a question of time for evolution to create complex and intelligent life forms in that the systems it creates reflects their environment better and better.

In modern society we constantly witness how something more intelligent develops out of something less intelligent. Everywhere human beings are in the process of developing more intelligent solutions than the solutions already known.

One special aspect of this work is the scientific uncovering of the detailed nature of the solutions that were created by nature itself during the long process of evolution. It has become more and more evident, how unbelievably intelligent the systems of the living organisms really are.

3.7 The Natural Constants

The natural constants that define our universe could theoretically be determined in millions of different ways. And only one of these seems to be compatible with life — at least in the form that we know it — and that is precisely the one that is realized on our universe.

---

[7]Popper's criticism of Plato's philosophy also appears unfair. The Platonic concern for insight in that which is good drives a positive development.

According to the argument from intelligent design, this determination of the natural constants is best be explained as the result of an intelligent design of the universe. It appears designed with a purpose, to support life, and not the result of a random selection of the values of the constants. It is unbelievably unlikely that the universe should have exactly those values that enable the emergence of life and nevertheless that were the constants it received. The most natural explanation why the constants obtained these values is that the universe was designed in this way so that it can develop and support life.

In this way the God of intelligent design is similar to the deontological God of the enlightenment: God the great mathematician that created the world according to his great mathematical design. The difference is that the idea of intelligent design directly involves the idea of a purpose. That which makes the design intelligent is that it is a solution of the very difficult problem of creating life in the universe.

The observation, that the world was created according to mathematical and thus apparently intelligent principles is very old. The claim of intelligent design, that it is based on scientific evidence in contrast to earlier arguments for God's existence, is simply not true. For example the ancient observation based idea that the planets move in circles — later with the emergence of modern natural science corrected to ellipses — is an early observation of something that has been interpreted as the result of God's intelligent work (design). After recognizing that this design actually is the result of natural laws the perspective shifts. Then God is not considered the designer of the concrete universe but of the mathematical laws that have generated the universe. In modern dress this becomes the idea that God has given the natural constants their specific values.

However, the reference to the value of the natural constants in the argument from intelligent design is constructed in a way that basically demonstrates the opposite of what is intended, because it actually presupposes an evolutionary perspective on the emergence of life. It assumes that intelligence can develop out of matter in at least one kind of world — ours. This is so because the argument is based on the presupposition that when the natural constants that define our universe are determined in a specific way, then intelligent life can emerge — i.e. evolve — in this universe. It can emerge out of a situation in which there is no life. If the natural constants have different values then life — or life as we know it — cannot emerge. But, that is precisely what scientific naturalism means, when it claims that life is the result of an evolutionary process.

The basic question of the debate is whether life can develop naturally as supposed in scientific naturalism or whether it presupposed a transcendent de-

Figure 3.6: The elliptic tracks of the planets seem to look designed.

signer, a super intelligent God.

However, the natural constants are relevant only because they are used to explain the nature of the developing universe. The special setting of the constants is used to explain why the universe developed in the way we know. By accepting the idea of explaining the development by reference to natural constants, one accepts the form of explanation of the development of the universe as promoted by the naturalist scientific outlook.

If one rejects the theory of evolution and claims that life was created by, for instance, God's intervention in the development of the universe, then the development of the universe was not a result of the value of the natural constants. Then the natural constants would not play a decisive role in our explanation and could not be used in the argument from intelligent design either.

Furthermore then one would not have a deontological God but an intervening unpredictable God and an unpredictable universe. Then there would be no design of the universe, because the universe was subject to God's will and intervention at any given moment. This kind of God is not incompatible with the argument from intelligent design at all.

We cannot say — at least not now — if the specific values of the basic natural constants are a kind of coincident or if they are the result of a deeper logic. Nor can we say if there — for instance — exist an infinite set of universes, each with a different setting of the natural constants. However, the fact that we find ourselves in a universe with the special setting of the natural constants, that enables the universe to support life, is not surprising.

We lack any understanding why a possible God would want to create precisely this universe. The argument from intelligent design does not help us. The idea, that God loves his creation, and that he is particularly fond of human beings, may be very nice, but it lacks any evidence.

3.8 The inclusive concept of the world

Design, intelligence and purpose are concepts that characterize phenomena that exist within a world where they are used to analyze and solve problems. Problems and solutions also can only exist in the context of a world. Outside the frame of a world they make no sense.

The concept of world has a special character. As soon as one imagines that there is something outside the world, the world automatically is enlarged to include this phenomenon. The concept of world is an all-inclusive concept. One can only put something outside its border by enlarging its very border to include it again.[8]

When, for instance, a person claims that the universe started with the Big Bangm then immediately questions arise, such as: what the Big Bag is, how it happened, what started it, and what was before the Big Bang, before the start of our universe.

Every answer to such question involves an enlargement of our notion of the world. When for instance we say that the world was created by the Big Bang by the explosion of a singularity, then we have of course pointed in the direction of a cause of the universe, but at the same time we have enlarged the notion of our world in that it now includes the idea of a singularity that existed before the Big Bang. In this way the concept of world is all-inclusive. It automatically swallows everything which we put outside it. If there is only the faintest relation between the world and something outside it, then automatically it becomes part of the world. If the world was created not by an exploding

---

[8]Compare K. Jaspers' (1883-1969) concept of the all-encompassing (*das Umgreifende*) for instance in *Vernunft und Existenz*, (1935). For the inherent philosophical problems in dualism see for instance Passmore (1961).

singularity but by an intelligent designing God, then he would automatically become part of the world.

This is why the very imagination of God is part some religious *world* views. To the religious person, God is not simply something outside the world, something transcendent. Then he would not be important. God interacts with his world. He creates it. He interferes with it. He communicates with his believers and ensures they receive his messages as to what to do and how to live. And he judges people and rewards or punishes them. If he did not do such things, if he was just a transcendent phenomenon standing in no relation to the world, then the concept of God would be uninteresting. What happens in dualist religions is that the world is subdivided in an Earthly world and a Heavenly world. Still there is a total world containing Heaven and Earth because there are supposed to be important connections between the two. They are joined in the religious world view and one may go from the one to the other. If they were not connected, there would be no point in the heavenly world. Thus we always have an inclusive concept of the World. We may subdivide it in local sections — say the Earthly world, or the windows-world, or the female world etc. All these sub-worlds are inclusive in their way. But the world as such is all-inclusive. Therefore it enables our understanding to develop further and further and cross previous boundaries.

If we want to stop explanation, then we introduce the inexplicable — such as God the designer — and let it be the explanation of something we do not understand. To claim that this is the final true explanation of the setting of the natural constants, the creation of the DNA or the nanomachines is in reality to claim that we shall never get any understanding of these questions. We cannot explain anything be reference to God. If he exists, then he is far too mysterious for us to obtain any understanding by reference to him.

3.9 Creation of the world — intelligently designed by human beings

There have been many intelligently designed visions of the creation of the world. All of them suffer from the problem of using the immanent concepts to vision the transcendent. The argument from intelligent design does this more than most other philosophical arguments for the existence of God.

Some of these visions are embedded in — or are the foundation of — mythological and religious beliefs. When for instance the Bible, the book of Genesis, tells that it took God 6 days to create the world, then we have a problem with understanding what 6 days is at a time before there are days,

Figure 3.7: The creator is busy. From Michelangelo's "Genesis", 1508-1512.

hours, and seconds, before there are watches, before there are atoms, before there is any time at all?

Some visions are expressed in art, as for instance Michelangelo's great work, *Genesis*, on the ceiling of the Sistine Chapel. Here God the creator is a busy man flying around in a space with his accompanying angels creating everything. Again this is all too anthropomorphic. Intelligent design is a vision that is man made.

Some of these visions have a philosophical, conceptual nature. Some of the problems discussed above are illustrated in the earliest known philosophical thoughts on the creation. The *Brhadaranyaka Upanishad (Great Forest Book)* from about 800 BCE describes the creation of the world as follows:

1. In the beginning there was in this world the Self (Atman)
alone in the form of a person
He looked around and saw nothing but himself.
Then he said: "I am"
This was the first thing he said.
In this way the name "I" was created. ... ...

2. He was afraid.
Therefore, a person who is alone is afraid.
Thus the One thought to himself:

"Since nothing but myself exists, of what am I afraid?"
Then his fear disappeared. What should he be afraid of?
It is obvious that fear emerges from an Other.

3. He had no pleasures.
Therefore, a person who is alone, he has no pleasure.
Thus he desired an Other.
He was as big as a man and a woman who embrace.
He caused this self to divide in two pieces.
From this emerged husband and wife. ... ...

5. He knew:
"I am this which is created. Because I emanated it all from myself."
Thus creation was done. ... ...

The very first line illustrates the problem that the concept of the world is all-inclusive: The creator, the One, the Self, Atman, is not positioned outside the world. In the *Upanishad* the solution to this problem is to reduce the original world to the Self, Atman. The *Upanishad* is clearly aware of this all-inclusive nature of the concept of the world. It sticks to the monism — even after creation it maintains the idea of there being only one world, which therefore must be identified with the absolute Self. 2500 years later, Spinoza creates great impact on western philosophy with a similar monistic logic.

In §2 fear is dismissed as absurd when there is no other. In §3 the *Upanishad* ascribes a wish for pleasure to the One, the Creator, God. One cannot avoid feeling puzzled how this craving for pleasure happened. What is wrong with being a perfect being? The *Upanishad* here implicitly draws from the pleasure involved in procreation — i.e. it imposes an immanent perspective on the absolute. The paragraphs try to give a deep explanation of the meaning of the basic of life: §1 concerns the self, §2 concerns fear and §3 concerns pleasure. However as a historical explanation or the origin of the universe this form of anthropomorphism violates the conditions for using the concepts of self, fear and pleasure. The author of the *Upanishad* tries to use this paradoxical situation dialectically by making creation a process that solves this paradox by creating a world. — However, the *Upanishad* avoids the dualist trap, which still bothers Judaism and Christianity.

All the intelligent designs of the world we know have one thing in common: They are all human. This includes the argument from design. Their merits are not their rationality but rather their visionary skills.

Figure 3.8: Boesch: "Creation of the world" — from the Triptych, 1500.

Chapter 4

The designed water flow through a plant leaf

Peder A. Tyvand
Department of Mathematical Sciences and Technology
Norwegian University of Life Sciences
P.O. Box 5003
1432 Ås
Norway

Abstract

A continuum model for the macroscopic water flow in plant leaves was introduced by Tyvand (1982). It is based on the conservation of mass and momentum and the continuum hypothesis. In the present work this continuum model is interpreted in the context of Intelligent Design (ID).

4.1 Introduction

The flow of water through plant leaves is of vital importance for the life on our planet. The production of organic matter on land takes place in the leaves of plants, through photosynthesis. No such production would be possible without the flow of water through each leaf. In this article we will identify correlations between the shape of a leaf and the geometry of its dominating veins. These correlations may be interpreted as resulting from Intelligent Design (ID). These correlations are holistic in the sense that they consider the leaf with its system of primary veins as an integrated unity. The control of the primary vein geometry involves the whole leaf and its contour shape, and cannot be regarded as a local phenomenon.

Darwinian evolution has always had the life of animals as its focus. This is a biased view in the sense that animal life is not a self-sufficient form of life. It is a dependent form of life, based on consumption of organic material supported by plants. The animal digestion of organic material implies a degradation that reduces the amount of oxygen in the atmosphere, and simultaneously increases the amount of carbon dioxid.

Plant life based on photosynthesis assembles and delivers organic material to the animal kingdom to remedy its degradations. By photosynthesis organic material is being built up. As an essential by-product the amount of oxygen in the atmosphere is being increased, and the amount of carbon dioxid is being reduced. The leaves are the organs of the plants that are responsible for most of this constructive process that all other land-based life depends on. Of all the processes that occur in a plant leaf, its throughflow of water is the most important one from a quantitative point of view. It is impossible to estimate its qualitative importance, compared with the active elements of the photosynthesis such as the collecting of photons and the intake of carbon dioxid. The photosynthesis could not take place without transport of water through a leaf. The importance of the water throughflow is seen when the water supply is scarce so the leaf suffers from drought stress that eventually may cause its death.

Discussions of evolution versus ID should not continue to be narrowly occupied with the animal kingdom. The debate should broaden and become more oriented toward plants and their photosynthesis. One phenomenon that will then immediately catch the attention is the water transport through plants.

A huge literature is devoted to water in connection with plants. However, the traditional study of water transport through plants has not focussed on one single leaf. On one hand, the large-scale water flow through the whole plant has been studied.[1] The following concepts are central in this study of macroscopic water throughflow: The uptake of water in the unsaturated root zone, the concept of water potential and the cohesion hypothesis. On the other hand,

---

[1] Sutcliffe (1968).

one has also studied the small-scale water flow through single stomata.[2] In recent years there has been a rapidly growing interest in the water flows in the vein networks of a single leaf.[3]

4.2 Physical principles

There are three basic physical principles governing the flow of water through plants:

      (i) Conservation of mass
      (ii) Conservation of momentum
      (iii) Conservation of energy

These three principles are generally established as governing principles for all fluid flow. We will apply a fourth principle that is very important for the mathematical description of fluid flow:

      (iv) The continuum hypothesis

The continuum hypothesis says that we may overlook the molecular scales of motion and work on a length scale where the averaged flow parameters can be taken as continuous functions of space and time. The density, the pressure and the three velocity components (U,V,W) are then assumed to be continuous functions of the three Cartesian coordinates (x,y,z) and time t. Here (U,V,W) are defined as the velocity components in the x, y and z direction.

Historically, the formulation of the continuum hypothesis rests on the analytical geometry founded by Descartes (1596-1650) and the differential calculus developed by Newton (1643-1727) and Leibniz (1646-1716). The mathematical formulation of fluid flow assuming the continuum hypothesis was first given by Euler (1707-1783). The continuum hypothesis offers very accurate description of flows in single fluids like water and air for pressures of order of magnitude comparable with ordinary atmospheric pressures. The continuum hypothesis is the conceptual basis of modern meteorology and oceanography, as well as many other branches of science and technology.

The usual physical quantity for validating the continuum hypothesis is the density. The density in a point is defined by means of a Representative Elementary Volume (REV). We take the REV as a cube with of volume L^3 and

---

[2] Willmer and Fricker (1996).
[3] See Bohn et al. (2002), Zwieniecki et al. (2002), Cochard et al. (2004) and the review article by Sack and Holbrook (2006). The present paper is based on an earlier theoretical paper Tyvand (1982).

centre in the point (x,y,z) under consideration. The crucial point is the definition of the length scale L of a REV. We define L to be as small as it possibly can be in order to filter out of the small-scale fluctuations of density. The continuum hypothesis is then valid if L is sufficiently small compared with all length scales of the flow.

In gas dynamics for the upper atmosphere of the earth, the continuum hypothesis breaks down when the gas density becomes so small that the length scale L of the REV becomes comparable or larger than the relevant length scale for the gas flow. The essential parameter for evaluating the continuum hypothesis in a gas is the Knudsen number. It is defined as the ratio of the molecular mean free path length to a representative physical length scale. The number is named after the Danish physicist Martin Knudsen (1871-1949). The Knudsen number is useful for determining whether statistical mechanics or the continuum mechanics formulation of fluid mechanics should be used: If the Knudsen number is near or greater than one, the mean free path of a molecule is comparable to a length scale of the problem, and the continuum assumption of fluid mechanics is no longer a good approximation. In this case statistical methods must be used. (Taken from http://www.wikipedia.org.)

4.3 The porous medium model of a leaf

So far, our discussion on the continuum hypothesis is concerned with the case of a single fluid. The discussion becomes more complicated when there are several fluids involved, or fluids in combination with solid material. In a plant leaf we will consider the dry part of the leaf tissue as a solid material, in contact with and penetrated by liquid water. We discuss the continuum hypothesis for this mixture of approximately stagnant solid tissue and slowly moving liquid water. We are then disregarding the flow of air components that are involved. The surrounding air is contributing to the photosynthesis by the net transport of carbon dioxid into the leaf and the net transport of oxygen out of the leaf, through the stomata in the leaf.

We disregard gas transport only as far as the components of air are concerned. We take into account the full mass transport of water, no matter whether it is present as vapour or in liquid phase. However, in the mathematical description of the water flow, we will assume that it consists only of liquid water.

The continuum hypothesis for fluid flow in between a solid material was first applied by the Frenchman Henri Darcy (1803-1858). He formulated what is now called Darcy's law for fluid flow in a porous medium, which can be expressed qualitatively as follows:

The resistance force for fluid flow through a porous medium is proportional to the fluid velocity

The solid material that surrounds the flowing fluid is called a porous medium. Darcy's law in its original form assumes that the flow is saturated, which means that the pores in the solid material is filled completely by just one fluid. Moreover, Darcy's law assumes that the solid porous medium is at rest, and the fluid velocity is measured relative to this stagnant solid medium. However, in a porous medium the continuum hypothesis enters the problem on a much greater length scale than in a flow of pure fluid. See the standard textbook on flows in porous media by Bear [4]. The Representative Elementary Volume (REV) will have a length scale that is somewhat greater than the size of the diameter of a pore where the fluid is flowing. Above the density was identified as the crucial physical quantity for deciding the length scale L for the REV. In general this does not work for a porous medium, because it might happen that the solid and the fluid have almost the same density.

The key quantity that is used for defining the REV in a porous medium is the porosity n. The porosity of the porous medium is defined as the fraction of a volume that is not occupied by the solid material. In saturated flow, the porosity n is defined as the fraction of a volume that is occupied by fluid. Let us explain how the porosity $n(x,y,z)$ is defined according to the continuum hypothesis. First we choose a point (x,y,z), and consider a surrounding cube of volume L^3 with its centre in (x,y,z). We start increasing the length scale L from zero and up. As long as L is very small, the value of $n(x,y,z)$ will be either close to zero or close to one. The value of n will be close to zero if the considered point (x,y,z) in the porous medium is occupied by the solid phase, and L is so small that most of the surrounding material in the cube is solid as well. On the other hand, the value of n will be close to one if the considered point (x,y,z) in the porous medium is occupied by the fluid phase, and L is so small that most of the surrounding material in the cube is fluid as well. When we increase L, the average of n over the cube volume will converge reasonably well to a common value that does not depend on whether the point (x,y,z) was chosen to be in the solid phase or in the fluid phase. If the smallest possible value for L to get this converged average is smaller than the smallest length scale of the average flow, then the continuum hypothesis is valid, and we can work with Darcy's law or extensions of it.

It is not obvious that the porous medium description is reasonably accurate for a plant leaf. The REV based on porosity will not be very small, which in-

---

[4] Bear (1972)

dicates that only the flow in the system of major veins can be included by such a continuum description. Moreover, the application of the purely mechanical Darcy's law will lead to the neglect of biochemical forces due to osmosis. Osmosis is a very important phenomenon governing the local flow through the membranes on the cell level, but it may give negligible contribution to the force balance integrated over a REV.

We will apply the continuum hypothesis for the large-scale flow of water in a plant leaf, and take only mechanical forces into account. Out of the three basic principles that govern the water flow through plants, the conservation of energy will not be relevant for our mathematical model. This is because we will assume that the water density ρ is constant. We are left with the two basic physical principles governing the flow of water through plants:

(i) Conservation of mass
(ii) Conservation of momentum

We will now formulate these two principles mathematically according to the continuum hypothesis. Many leaves have shapes that are curved in space, which can be accounted for. In the present paper we will only consider plane leaves, so we introduce the Cartesian coordinates x and y in the plane of the leaf. Time is denoted by t. In order to formulate mass conservation, we must introduce the transpiration $T(x,y,t)$. The transpiration is the volume of water per unit of leaf area and time that is lost from the leaf surface, mostly through the stomata. The transpiration in a point (x,y) on the leaf sums up the loss of water from both sides of the leaf.

Conservation of mass is then given by the equation

$$\frac{\partial u}{\partial x} + \frac{\partial v}{\partial y} = s(x,y,t) - T(x,y,t), \qquad (4.1)$$

valid for the porous medium continuum model of a leaf. The function $s(x,y,t)$ describes the source input of water to the leaf, either from a node point or from a dominating mid-vein. The "velocity field" in eq. (1) has components u and v in the x and y directions. More precisely, u and v are called the x and y components of the specific flux vector. Let us give its precise definition: Assume $U(x,y,z,t)$ and $V(x,y,z,t)$ are the local pore velocities, and the function $d(x,y)$ describes the thickness of the leaf. Then the flow field (u,v) is defined by integrating over the thickness of the leaf as follows

$$[u,v] = \int_0^{d(x,y)} [U(x,y,t), V(x,y,t)] dz \qquad (4.2)$$

where $d(x,y)$ denotes the thickness of the leaf as a function of position. Note that the units of u and v are square meters per second.

Conservation of momentum is given by the classical Darcy's law for a homogeneous and isotropic porous medium, which may be written in local form as

$$(U,V) + \frac{k}{\mu}\left(\frac{\partial p}{\partial x}, \frac{\partial p}{\partial y}\right) = 0, \tag{4.3}$$

where k is the permeability of the porous medium, μ is the dynamic viscosity and p is the pressure. It is difficult to recognize eq. (3) as a conservation law for momentum. In general a momentum conservation equation will be of the vector form

$$\Delta(m\vec{v}) = \Sigma \vec{F} \Delta t, \tag{4.4}$$

expressing a balance between the change of momentum and the sum of force impulses. In a porous medium the velocity is so small that it is customary to neglect the momentum, so that the momentum equation reduces to a force balance

$$\Sigma \vec{F} = 0, \tag{4.5}$$

which is essentially Newton's first law. Darcy's law (3) expresses the balance between the pressure resultant force and viscous drag. Let us integrate eq. (3) over the leaf thickness to get Darcy's law in the form

$$(u,v) + \frac{K}{\mu}\left(\frac{\partial p}{\partial x}, \frac{\partial p}{\partial y}\right) = 0, \tag{4.6}$$

where a modified permeability factor K arises from the integration. It results from the integration of the pressure term over the leaf thickness, and will be assumed constant. We need a kinematic boundary conditions for the flow along the edge of the leaf. It is the condition of zero throughflow, which is written as

$$n_x u + n_y v = 0, \text{ along the leaf contour.} \tag{4.7}$$

Here we have introduced the unit normal vector (n_x, n_y) pointing out from the contour curve of the leaf. Condition (7) says that the leaf contour is a streamline for the flow field $(u(x,y), v(x,y))$. This means that we may redefine the leaf contour *a posteriori* so that it follows a streamline. Then the node point will be located at the border of the leaf. This is the common situation for monocotyledon leaves, where a system of parallel veins start out from a node point where the stem meets the leaf. Mathematically, only the fraction $(\Delta\alpha/(2\pi))$ of the total source gives input to a leaf where $\Delta\alpha$ is the starting angle between the two streamlines that define the contour of the leaf.

The boundary condition (7) also implies that the complete outflow from the leaf occurs from its surface, through the stomata. This is expressed by integrating eq. (1) over the leaf surface area A, giving

$$\int s(x,y,t)dA = \int T(x,y,t)dA, \qquad (4.8)$$

where we have applied the Gauss theorem (Kaplan 1991) and the boundary condition (7). Eq. (8) expresses the mass balance between the source influx of water and the total transpiration from the leaf surface.

The boundary value problem consists of eqs. (1) and (4) with the boundary condition (7), once the source function s and the leaf contour is specified. The transpiration enters only the mass conservation equation (1). For simplicity, we will hereafter assume that the transpiration is independent of space so that we have $T = T(t)$. This means that transpiration is considered uniform over the whole leaf surface at each instant. It is impossible to assume T independent of time. Indeed there is a strong time variation as the stomata open and close.

Here we must warn against a misinterpretation of our hydrodynamic leaf model. The assumption of spatially uniform transpiration $T = T(t)$ cannot be strictly valid locally at any instant, which implies that local short-time fluctuations must be filtered out from our continuum description. The point of our assumption of uniform transpiration is not that all stomata are opened and closed in a completely synchronized way. The point is rather that the complete surface of the leaf receives the same supply of water available for transpiration, so that the transpiration per unit area can possibly be uniformly distributed over the leaf area. The local osmotic transport at the lowest hierarchical level of veins may take care of the local short time fluctuations and filter them out so that the macroscopic flow that we consider can have spatially uniform transpiration.

With the simplifying assumption of uniform transpiration, we can in fact stretch the time coordinate to make the mathematical problem steady. Since transpiration is the only quantity with time variation, we can introduce a stretched time coordinate τ defined by

$$T(t)dt = T_0 d\tau. \qquad (4.9)$$

Here T_0 is an arbitrary reference transpiration, and its only purpose is to keep τ as a time coordinate. We may integrate eq. (9) to give a more explicit definition of the new time variable τ as

$$\tau = T_0^{-1} \int T(t)dt, \qquad (4.10)$$

where the origin of the time coordinate is left unspecified. When τ is taken as the new time variable, time cancels out completely from the boundary value problem represented by eqs. (1), (6)-(7). Conservation of mass is then given by the equation

$$\frac{\partial u}{\partial x} + \frac{\partial v}{\partial y} = s(x,y) - T, \qquad (4.11)$$

where T can now be taken as constant. Only the source distribution function $s(x,y)$ must be specified in each case, recalling that its integral over the leaf area A is equal to the product TA, from eq. (8). From Darcy's law (6) we eliminate the pressure to get the equation

$$\frac{\partial v}{\partial x} - \frac{\partial u}{\partial y} = 0 \qquad (4.12)$$

which means that the flow field is irrotational. If the flow had been rotational, one would have seen spiral vein shapes in nature.

4.4 The circular leaf

The simplest possible case is the flat circular leaf with radial veins from a central node. This is a relevant model for shield-formed leaves. Two examples are the popular summer flower *Tropaeolum majus* and the water plant *Brasenia schreberi*. Let us give the mathematical solution for this case, because it is an instructive starting point for developing more general solutions. The radial velocity v_r is simply

$$v_r = \frac{S}{2\pi r} - r\frac{T}{2}, \quad 0 \leq r < a, \qquad (4.13)$$

where $r = (x^2 + y^2)^{1/2}$ is the radial coordinate and a is the radius of the circular leaf given by the mass balance relation

$$S = \pi a^2 T, \qquad (4.14)$$

where S is the volume flux that enters the leaf from the leaf stem at the node point where all the primary veins come from. The assumption that the influx of water is concentrated in a node point located in the origin means that we have chosen as the source function

$$s(x,y) = S\delta(x)\delta(y), \qquad (4.15)$$

where δ denotes the Dirac delta function.

4.5 The holism of an elliptic problem

In our previous paper where this continuum model for water flow in a leaf was introduced[5], we considered both a point source and various line source distributions for $s(x,y)$. The point source corresponds to a node point where the stem meets with all the primary veins of the leaf. Line sources correspond to one dominating mid-vein from which a series of primary veins branch out. Whether the point source or the line source model is relevant depends on the species of the plant. The point source model is relevant for the leaves of monocotyledon plants. Most dicotyledon plants have leaves with one dominating mid-vein. In our model, this would be represented by a line source. However, in the present article we will consider only the point source. This is the simplest case where the inflow of water comes from one singular point that is placed in the origin, according to eq. (15).

The importance of starting with the above example of a circular leaf is that both the source flow $(S/(2\pi r))$ and the transpiration flow $(-rT/2)$ will retain their mathematical form in the general case. All we have to do in order to formulate the general problem is to rewrite the source flow and the transpiration flow in Cartesian coordinates and introduce an additional third type of flow called the adaptation flow. The role of the adaptation flow is to adapt the whole flow pattern for the primary veins to the contour shape of the leaf, while the law of least resistance for the flow is still valid.

For the case of a point source in the origin, the general form of the velocity field is

$$(u,v) = \left(\frac{S}{2\pi(x^2+y^2)^{1/2}} - \frac{T}{2}\right)(x,y) + \left(\frac{\partial \phi}{\partial x}, \frac{\partial \phi}{\partial y}\right), \quad (4.16)$$

where we have introduced a potential $\phi(x,y)$ that represents the adaptation flow. The form (16) is necessary to satisfy the constraint of irrotational flow (12), Inserting eq. (16) into the mass balance equation (11) gives Laplace's equation

$$\frac{\partial^2 \phi}{\partial x^2} + \frac{\partial^2 \phi}{\partial y^2} = 0, \quad (4.17)$$

governing the adaptation flow, with an associated boundary condition (7) of the Neumann type.

We see that the mathematical problem that governs the adaptation flow is an elliptic problem. The nature of elliptic boundary value problems is that the solution everywhere depends on the conditions specified along the whole boundary. There is no limited domain of influence as in hyperbolic problems,

---

[5] Tyvand (1982).

or a finite signal speed as in parabolic diffusion problems. Every point in the flow domain is influenced by the conditions along the entire boundary. If the primary veins of a leaf are governed by an elliptic boundary value problem, they will all be tied together in an interdependence with the shape of the whole leaf. An elliptic boundary value problem for a leaf vein system may be interpreted as a quantitative ID structure. Strictly speaking though, these strong correlations between leaf shape and flow pattern only indicate the causality of ID, but do not logically imply this causality. Darwinism tends to cross the border between correlation and causation. A standard Darwinian mistake is to assume that the common genetic coding medium of DNA (correlation) implies a continuous natural descent from common ancestors (causality).

The alternative continuum models that exist for leaf venation are not based on elliptic boundary-value problems. Meinhardt[6] and Mitchison[7] have studied reaction-diffusion models. These are boundary-value problems of the parabolic type with a finite signal propagation velocity. The underlying assumption is that the veins in a leaf is a Turing structure[8]. A Turing structure is a structure that arises spontaneously due to instability in a nonlinear coupled reaction-diffusion system. Turing models for plant leaves are based on the principles of autocatalysis and lateral inhibition, but are not representative for the main system of veins in a leaf. Undoubtedly, there are physical phenomena that actually follow the principles of autocatalysis and lateral inhibition. A well-known example is the lightning in a thunderstorm[9]. A Turing structure is not designed, but is a result of self-organization.

Our elliptic boundary-value problem for the adaptation flow gives a correlation between the contour of a plant leaf and the geometric pattern of its primary veins. This correlation can in principle be expressed by Green's third identity in potential theory[10]

$$\phi(x,y) = \frac{1}{2\pi} \int_C \left(\log\left(\frac{1}{r}\right) \frac{\partial \phi}{\partial n} - \phi \frac{\partial}{\partial n} \log\left(\frac{1}{r}\right) \right) ds. \qquad (4.18)$$

This integral formula gives the value of a harmonic function $\phi(x,y)$ in any interior point (x,y) inside the given closed contour C. The normal derivative at the contour C is denoted by $\partial/\partial n$. The integration is performed over a line element ds expressed by the dummy coordinates (x',y'). The radial variable in the integral is defined by $r = ((x-x')^2 + (y-y')^2)^{1/2}$. Green's third identity

---

[6] Meinhardt (1976).
[7] Mitchison (1980).
[8] Turing (1952).
[9] Meinhardt (1982).
[10] Kaplan (1991).

gives the value of the function in any interior point as a boundary integral that involves the function $\phi(x',y')$ and its normal derivative along the contour. In the present problem we identify the function $\phi(x,y)$ as the adaptation flow potential. When we insert eq. (16) into the boundary condition (7), we see that the normal derivative of ϕ is specified along the contour. To proceed from here we first need to determine the function ϕ itself along the contour. This is done by solving an integral equation that is also called Green's second identity. We omit the details here and refer to Kaplan[11]. Once we have solved this equation we know both the adaptation flow potential ϕ and its normal derivative along the entire contour. Then we know all terms in Green's third identity (18), and can perform the contour integration for any fixed interior point (x,y) to find the value of $\phi(x,y)$ that determines the whole macroscopic water flow through the leaf.

The general correlation between the shape of a leaf and its macroscopic water flow that is expressed by Green's third identity (18) has no Darwinian explanation, and can be interpreted as a quantitative ID result. This is significant because ID is often accused of being merely qualitative in its propositions. The correlation between leaf shape and flow expressed by Green's third identity is unique except for one thing. The source inflow that enters eq. (16) represents generally a source distribution that will affect the normal derivative of ϕ through the boundary condition (7). The source distribution must be given a priori, so that it corresponds to the way the inflow of water from the stem is organized in the type of leaf that we consider.

The specification of the source distribution depends of the type of plant that we consider. Some leaves are best represented by a point source. These are typical monocotyledon leaves that have one node point which is the common origin of all major veins. Other leaves must be represented by a line source. These are the typical dicotyledon leaves that have one dominating mid-vein that all the major veins branch out from.

Once an elliptic boundary-value problem applies to the water flow in a leaf, Green's third identity is a holistic and quantitative design principle. It relies on the existence of an adaptation flow. The concept of adaptation flow is not relevant for all leaves, but only for those with a reasonably smooth contour curve. A number of dicotyledon plants have leaves with corrugated contour, to which the flow model presented here does not apply. We consider leaves with smooth contour curve. The easiest way of producing predictions of leaf shapes, is to construct an adaptation flow by means of functions of a complex variable, and see what kinds of leaf contours and flow patterns that will result.

---

[11] Kaplan (1991).

This indirect solution procedure is the most efficient method to explore the design principle and compare its results with real leaves. It is better than the direct method where a leaf contour is given, and one tries to find the harmonic function by numerical solution of a Neumann problem for the adaptation flow.

4.6 Computations of theoretical leaves

We will show two computed examples of theoretical leaves with a single node point. Above we have sketched a direct method of solution: Specifying the leaf shape and the source distribution and solve Laplace's equation for the flow field by Green's identities. A convenient way of solving the problem is the indirect method: To start with assuming a given harmonic function for the adaptation flow, and compute the associated streamline pattern and leaf contour.

We will apply the indirect method, and compute streamlines numerically by MATHEMATICA. The advantage of this method is that we know the exact macroscopic flow, and that we get high accuracy in the computations. The disadvantage is that we cannot prescribe the exact leaf shape, and we have to approximate the shape that we want by trial and error. This is very cumbersome because the leaf contour is very sensitive to small parameter changes. In our theoretical solutions, we will exclude a fraction of the source, so that the node point will be located at the boundary.

In Figure 4.1 we have chosen an adaptation potential given as a uniform vertical flow plus an exponential function. The leaf shape and flow pattern that it gives resembles the leaves of the forest spring flower *Maianthemum bifolium*. Note that the streamlines are tangents to the leaf contour, and there is just one stagnation point where the total velocity is zero. This stagnation point is located at the leaf apex where all the streamlines meet. It is a stagnation point that attracts and collects all the streamlines. We call it a stagnation point of the first kind. This type of stagnation point is very common in nature, especially among monocotyledons like lilies and orchids.

There is a second kind of stagnation point, which repels or spreads the streamlines. It is not very common in nature, but the wetland plant *Sagittaria sagittifolia* is a splendid example. Figure 4.2 shows a simulation of a theoretical leaf in comparison with a photograph of a real leaf of this species. This theoretical leaf has been constructed by the computer program COMSOL MULTIPHYSICS which solves the differential equation with the appropriate boundary conditions by the finite element method. The theoretical leaf shape was specified as an arrow consisting of four straight lines, and the source (node point) for the water flow is located in the central concave corner of the arrow.

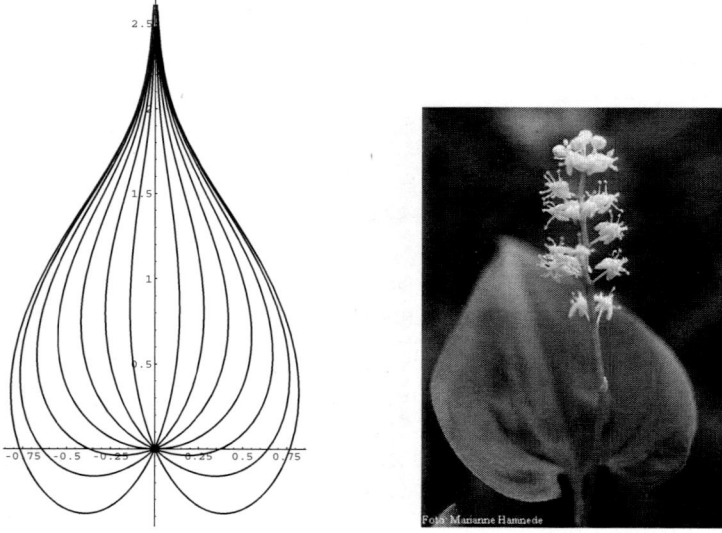

Figure 4.1: Theoretical and real leaves with one stagnation point of the first kind.

The arrow-shaped leaf of Figure 4.2 has a stagnation point of the first kind in each of the three apex points 1, 2 and 3. Moreover it has two stagnation points of the second kind in the points 4 and 5. We note that the streamlines that meet the stagnation points 4 and 5 are almost straight lines out from the node point, directed normally to the leaf contour. The location of the stagnation points and the flow pattern is in good agreement with the system of primary veins in the real leaves of *Sagittaria sagittifolia*.

In both figures we have taken constant angular increment between two neighbouring streamlines. This implies that the area between each pair of streamlines is constant, because the leaf transpiration is assumed spatially constant.

4.7 Conclusions

The present paper is an updated presentation of an earlier work on water flow in a single plant leaf (Tyvand 1982). This work is now interpreted into the context of Intelligent Design (ID). The hydrodynamic flow model is based on conservation principles for the macroscopic flow, and the application of the continuum hypothesis where the leaf is considered as a porous medium.

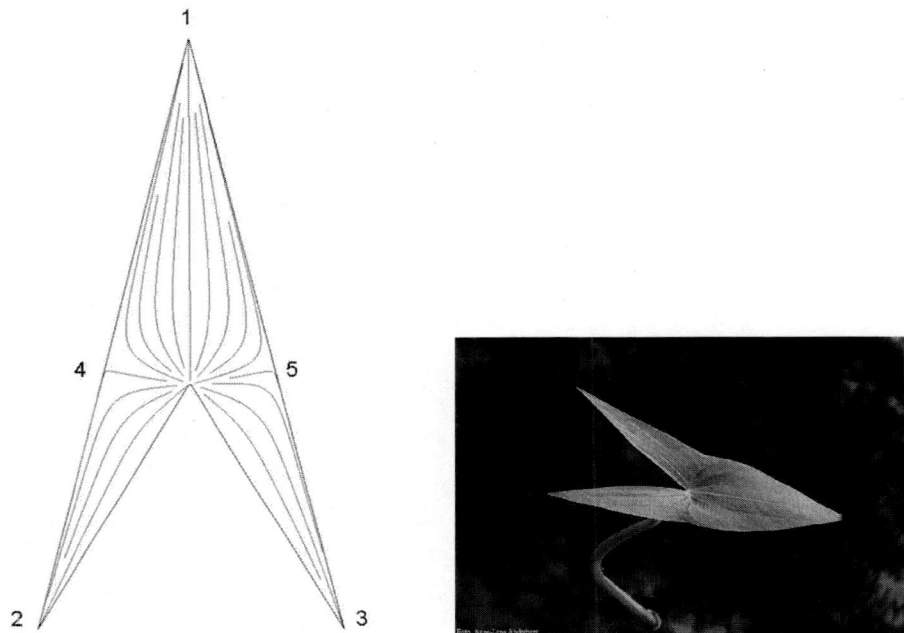

Figure 4.2: Theoretical and real leaves with stagnation points of the second kind.

Veins in a plant leaf are hierarchical. All veins at one level in the hierarchy have roughly the same diameter scale and the same length scale. They all receive water from the veins at the hierarchical level above. They all provide veins at the hierarchical level below with water. The highest level of veins receives water directly from the stem, and pressure (including suction due to cohesion) provides the dominating driving force. The lowest level of veins delivers water to the surrounding tissue, where osmosis provides the dominating driving force.

An important difference between the highest and the lowest hierarchical level of veins is that the highest-level veins are one-way tubes whereas the lowest-level veins form networks where the flow direction is not fixed and may change. This difference has to do with the different driving forces of the thickest and thinnest veins. The pressure-driven flow in the thickest veins has the direction from the source point at the leaf stem out towards the periphery of the leaf. Each of the thickest veins at the highest hierarchical level has a thickness that shrinks in the direction of the flow. The thinnest veins at the lowest hierarchical level tend to have constant average thicknesses. The network of these thinnest veins must be able to provide two-way osmotic transport to adjust to local fluctuations in the stomata opening rates and the water content in the tissue. When the driving force is osmotic, the flow direction in each element of the vein network must be arbitrary as it may change with time. With pressure as the only driving mechanism, the flow direction cannot change.

Because of the qualitative differences between pressure-driven and osmotic flows, there must be at least three levels in the hierarchy of venation in a plant leaf. One highest level, one lowest level, plus one level that is intermediate and provides the link between these other two. Kang and Dengler[12] studied the hierarchical levels in the leaves of *Arabidopsis thaliana*. From their work one may identify four distinct hierarchical levels of veins. The known theories of Turing structures disregard the notion of a hierarchy. There will be just one level of veins within a conventional Turing structure of self-organization. The primary veins in a leaf are not Turing structures. Only the lowest level of veins in a leaf may possibly be pure Turing structures. The water flow is important at all hierarchical levels, but is generally excluded from all models of Turing structures.

There are several inconsistencies in the reductionistic Turing models for leaf venation[13]. A virtual homogenous leaf without veins is assumed to exist before the diffusion process of self-organization starts from one end of the unstructured leaf. Such an unstructured leaf without veins is a reductionistic fiction without any empirical realism. The Turing models for venation disregard completely water transport, which is the quantitatively dominating phenomenon. As a result one will get veins that have spiral shapes that violate the principle of least resistance, being far from functional for efficient water supply. The present model is holistic and optimized with respect to transport and entropy production. Instead of disregarding the water transport, our design model is indeed based on the water throughflow through a leaf.

The veins in a plant leaf are constituted by two types of vascular tissue: xylem and phloem. The xylem is responsible for the outward water transport from the stem. The phloem is responsible for the transport of nutrients in the leaf. The present flow model is an averaged continuum model. Only a common average flow for the phloem and the xylem will be represented at the macroscopic length scales of the model. The xylem type of tissue dominates the pressure-driven veins at the highest hierarchical levels, while the phloem type of tissue enters the lower level where osmosis is important. The predictions

---

[12] Kang and Dengler (2004).
[13] Meinhardt (1976).

of the present model are concerned with the highest hierarchical levels where xylem is the dominating type of vascular tissue.

The role of genetics in the macroscopic water flow through a plant leaf has not been discussed explicitly here. Darwinian biology does not offer any understanding of this, since it has overlooked the fact that all vein systems in leaves are hierarchical. Darwinism does not even pose the right questions for understanding the genetic control behind leaf hydraulics. The reductionistic models of Turing structures for plant leaves[14] include only a vague link to genetics. The dynamic process of self-organization of the Turing structures is independent of genetics. Genetics can only play an implicit role in the frame behind this dynamics, by controlling which diffusive biochemical substances that are allowed to enter the stage and be involved in the dynamic processes. In a holistic ID model of a leaf, the macroscopic water balance must be governed by subtle interactions of many genes.

We have applied Darcy's law for the water flow through a plant leaf. Darcy's law is one example of a phenomenological law of least resistance. Laws for irreversible transport phenomena that are fully analogous to Darcy's law are Ohm's law of electric conduction and Fourier's law of heat conduction. The three phenomenological laws of Darcy, Ohm and Fourier postulate linear relationships between a flux and its driving gradient: From a mathematical point of view, these laws are essentially Taylor expansions that are truncated after one term only. In the present work we assume that the flux points in the direction of its driving gradient, which means that the medium that carries the flux is assumed isotropic. The three laws of Darcy, Ohm and Fourier express flows in the direction of least resistance, and it can be shown that they give minimum entropy production. For example, Perez[15] gave an analysis of the entropy production according to Ohm's law. Similar analyses can be given for Darcy's law and Fourier's law. These are well-known examples of Prigogine's postulate of minimum entropy production in non-equilibrium thermodynamics[16].

Our model for the macroscopic water throughflow in a leaf has the implication that entropy production is minimal. This is a constructional argument for the leaf, suitable for an ID interpretation. It has recently been argued that the principle of minimum entropy production also applies to photosynthesis in a plant leaf[17]. This gives two independent scientific reasons to assume that the leaves in nature are already to a great extent optimized as they enter the stage of existence. A view that is hereby emerging on the conditions for production

---

[14]Meinhardt (1982).
[15]Perez (2000).
[16]Prigogine (1967).
[17]Andriesse and Hollestelle (2001).

of organic material in a plant leaf is quite different from the conventional Darwinian view. This view is an ID view of a leaf based on holistic optimization principles both for the flow and the photosynthesis. The Darwinian concepts of mutations and selection may have only a secondary place, as they are disclosed as being void of explanatory power at the level of one single leaf. Darwinian processes have no correlation with the holistic principles of minimum entropy production. Darwinian processes do not have any governing influence on the overall shape of a leaf and its system of primary veins. These processes exist, but they may only enter the stage after the leaves have started to function and develop as a product of design. The clear indication of the present work is that the Darwinian processes in connection with plant leaves may serve merely as processes of degradation.

Chapter 5

To be or not to be intelligently designed – that's the question

Jörg Zeller
Aalborg University, Denmark

Over thirty-seven years ago, I learned of absolute proof that God exists. My studies lasted 2 1/2 years. I came to realize that I did not have to accept His existence "on faith." Since that time, science has learned much more and the "case" for God's existence has become far stronger than at any time in history. This booklet presents numerous absolute, immutable proofs that God *does* exist. After reading it, you will never again doubt the answer to this greatest of questions![1]

If people *refuse* to accept proof — evidence — *truth* — of the existence of God, there is absolutely nothing that can be said to erase their willful blindness. Remember, only the "fool has said in his heart, There is no God."[2]

---

[1] Pack (n.d.), "Does God Exist?" http://www.thercg.org/books/dge.html.
[2] Pack (n.d.), "Does God Exist?".

> Es mag wohl erlaubt sein, das Dasein eines Wesens von der höchsten Zulänglichkeit, als Ursache zu allen möglichen Wirkungen, anzunehmen, um der Vernunft die Einheit der Erklärungsgründe, welche sie sucht, zu erleichtern. Allein, sich so viel herauszunehmen, daß man so gar sage: ein solches Wesen existiert notwendig, ist nicht mehr die bescheidene Äußerung einer erlaubten Hypothese, sondern die dreiste Anmaßung einer apodiktischen Gewißheit; denn, was man als schlechthinnotwendig zu erkennen vorgibt, davon muß auch die Erkenntnis absolute Notwendigkeit bei sich führen.[3]

5.1 Are there absolute, immutable proofs that God does exist?

I must confess: My knowledge of the existing Intelligent Design (ID in the following) literature is very modest. So I don't know if all advocates of the idea of an intelligently designed world would agree with David C. Pack, "Pastor General" of "The Restored Church of God"[4] and a self-declared "*God-appointed, official 'Apostle' of the 21st century*"[5], that they are able to present "*absolute, immutable proofs that God does exist*".[6] I don't know either if all ID-proponents are prepared to call those people "fools" who believe that there is no evidence or proof for the existence of a divine entity. It is true, Kant (1998) considered it permissible to suppose the existence of a supreme entity as the cause of all possible effects in order to facilitate the finding of the unity of all those reasons that reasoning is searching for. However, he judged the claim that such an entity necessarily exists a *"cheeky presumption of an apodictic certainty"* (ibid., 684).

Whether presumptuous or part of a serious search for argumentation, the purpose of ID is:[7]

> to investigate whether or not existing empirical evidence implies that life on Earth must have been designed by an intelligent agent or agents. *William A. Dembski*, one of intelligent design's leading proponents, has stated that the fundamental claim of intelligent design is that "there are

---

[3] Kant (1998).
[4] cf. http://www.thercg.org/inside_rcg.html
[5] cf. http://www.exitsupportnetwork.com/artcls/Pack.htm
[6] http://www.thercg.org/books/dge.html
[7] according to http://da.wikipedia.org/wiki/Intelligent_design

natural systems that cannot be adequately explained in terms of undirected natural forces and that exhibit features which in any other circumstance we would attribute to intelligence." [8]

The same source describes Dembski's proposal in the following way:

> According to Dembski, the scientific study of nature reveals evidence of design, and opposes what he regards as mainstream science's commitment to "atheistic" materialism or naturalism, which he believes rules out "Intelligent Design" *a priori*. His main proposal is that specified complexity, a type of information, is the hallmark of an intelligent designer.[9]

Whether on the basis of divine appointment or of reasoning about empirical evidence, ID-proponents apparently use arguments that in some aspects resemble Immanuel Kant's 1762 (1916) considerations about "The only possible argument for a demonstration of the existence of God"[10]. The core of Kant's 1762 considerations concerns the logic of the modal concepts of possibility, necessity, and contingency and their meaning function for the concepts of stability (sentential meaning) and existence. It is known that Kant 1762 and 1998 favours a cosmological argument for a divine primary cause and rejects any form of ontological argument.

Kant is, however, aware that the basis for the cosmological argument, the principle of causality, doesn't *prove*[11] the existence of a divine entity. He therefore supports the causality argument by a consideration that is in part modal-logical, in part metaphysical, and in part semantic. In this way he unifies questions about the semantic, the metaphysical and empirical or, as I suggest to call it, the informational meaning of the modalities.

According to Kant, to be possible means to be a predicate not in contradiction, i.e. compatible with the subject of the proposition. Possibility, thus, is the same as stability or meaningfulness. You can think and state everything, which is not in contradiction with itself. Of course, you can't infer existence from possibility, i.e. from statability or "thinkability". If you could, there would no longer be a difference between the thinkable/possible and the true/factual. By the same token there would no longer be a difference between

---

[8] Dembski (2004, p. 27).

[9] http://en.wikipedia.org/wiki/William_A._Dembski

[10] cf. Kant (1762)

[11] "It has ... been shown that the inference from the properties of things of the world to the existence and properties of the deity contains a good and beautiful argument though it never can reach the strength of a demonstration." Kant (1916, p. 231), my translation. JZ.

the possible and the contingent, i.e. between the possibly and the factually true or between the imaginable and the existing.

Kant's rejection of the ontological argument is based on the fundamental epistemological importance of sticking to this difference. Even if it should be possible to think or imagine a most perfect entity (Descartes) or to think *"that than which no greater can be conceived"*[12], it wouldn't follow that such an entity exists. For instance, it is compatible with the concept of a right-angled triangle that it has two legs being 10 meter long and a hypotenuse 14,1421356 meter long, though this proves nothing about the existence of such a triangle. You have to find, i.e. to look at, touch, and measure an existing triangle to check out if it has the above property or not. Thus, to find an existing triangle, experience is required. On the basis of Kant's epistemology stressing the principal difference between concept (thinkability, meaning) and experience (sensibility, sensible contact with the real), this is true of every entity – in particular of a divine entity.

The difference between possibility or meaningfulness and existence notwithstanding, Kant 1762 considers it to be reasonable to conclude from possibility as a *consequence* onto the existence of a deity as a *reason* (cf. ibid., 225). If nothing at all would exist, Kant argues, nothing could be possible. It is therefore necessary that something exists in order to something else being possible. – To that, I agree: If the concept of possibility has any meaning, it is necessary that something exists which makes it possible that another thing can exist. However, I do not agree that it were possible to infer from the necessity of something existing onto the existence of a "necessary entity", i.e. an infinite, always and everywhere existing entity. From the necessity that something must exist in order to something being the case and therefore being thinkable and meaningful, it does not follow that an individual and unique thing must exist that is the basis (cause) of everything that has existed, exists, or can exist (in the future), i.e. the universe or reality. The necessary condition of something existing so that other things can be is already fulfilled by a finite and imperfect reality that doesn't a priori realize all possibilities. The necessity of something existing does not require a necessary existence. It suffices that there is something contingently.

Therefore, in my opinion, Kant's argument for a *cosmological* demonstration is not valid, since it is based on a conflation of the concepts of intentionality (meaningfulness), validity (inferentiality), and reality (sensibility). It is generally known that Kant 1998 only accepts this conflation in form of an idea, as a claim that is *reasonable*, i.e. in accordance with reason, but unable to be

---

[12] Anselm, cf. Wegener (2003).

confirmed by empirical evidence.

Let us have a closer look at why according to Kant all attempts of an *ontological* demonstration of a divine existence are invalid. Existence, Kant 1762 argued, is not a *predicate* or *concept* of anything. Predicates are possibilities. To say, that something (*S*) *is* predicate (*P*), means that *S* possibly is *P*, or that it is possible that *S* is *P*. It is crucial for the logic of modalities that it doesn't follow from *S*'s possibly *being P*, that *S really is P*. Thus, according to Kant the Anselmian and Cartesian trick – first suppose (think of, mean, intend) a divine entity as the most perfect or greatest being and then derive its existence as a part of its perfectness or greatness – doesn't hold. In so far as *"existence not at all is a predicate it isn't a predicate of perfectness either"*, Kant claims (ibid., 224). The invalidity of the inference from the possible as argument/reason to the existence as consequence doesn't, however, prohibit inferring the other way round, namely *"from the possibility of things as consequences to the existence of God as argument/reason"* (cf. ibid., 225). Kant's 1762 argument runs as follows:

> It is necessary that something exists so that some (other) thing can be (possible).
> If nothing at all would exist, nothing could be possible.
> The existing also is possible.
> Therefore: it is necessary that something exists.

Kant's next step is to argue that something necessarily existing means the same as the existence of a *necessary being* – because to exist necessarily is the same as to exist any time and any place, i.e. in eternity and everywhere. A being with the power to be always and everywhere must, of course, also be almighty and, if so, omniscient and so on[13]

In fact, Kant 1762 concedes that he is talking about *conditional* possibilities, i.e. about something that can be the case if/when something other is the case. To take an example: consciousness is possible if there exists a living being with functioning sense organs, nervous system and brain. The existence of such a living being is, however, only a *necessary* but not a *sufficient* condition of consciousness. Living beings with intact organs can be alive without being conscious of something.

Conditional possibility presupposes (necessarily, i.e. logically) something

---

[13] Kant 1762 (1916) formulates: *„Here it is investigated if something existing has to be supposed in order to something being possible and if this existing thing without which there is no inner possibility doesn't have such properties as we altogether connect with the concept of deity."* (ibid., 225, my transl.). Here, in my opinion, Kant transcends the borderline between logical and empirical necessity – the borderline that is crucial for his later (1998) transcendentalist epistemology of the interplay between experience and understanding.

being the case in order to be possible. This something is usually called the *cause* or one of a multiplicity of causes of the possible thing. That all there is or happens has to be caused by something, is, however, not a necessary, i.e. logical, but a metaphysical principle. Metaphysics concerns the constitution of reality. Metaphysicians design different models of the universe, and different metaphysical models are compatible with reality. For example, it is possible, i.e. not self-contradicting, to think that everything in the world is caused by another thing, but not that the whole world and reality itself is caused by another thing. Stephen Hawking (1998) mentions the possibility of a closed universe without beginning or ending. Such a world would just be and would make the existence of a transcendent creator unnecessary. In consequence, also Kant's 1762 *only possible argument for the demonstration of the existence of God*, the so-called cosmological argument, eventually boils down to the same sophism as the ontological argument – it may be reasonable but it isn't sound.

To make my own considerations about the reasonability of an intelligently designed world clearer, I will, in the following paragraphs, to begin with, look at some customary dictionary explanations of the words 'design' and 'intelligence' so as to catch a glimpse of what it means to say: something is intelligently designed. Next, I will consider a simple instance of an intelligently designed device and ask what it would mean if this device were designed to evolve in a similar manner as living beings on earth do. My argument will be that in an evolutionary world it makes no difference if it is intelligently designed or not. I will call this first part of my considerations my metaphysical argument. The second part deals with the question if there is a demarcation between knowledge and belief or not. My second argument will be that, if there is such a demarcation, then we can't know if the world is intelligently designed or not. I will call this my epistemological argument.

5.2 My metaphysical argument against intelligent design – the evolutionary alarm clock

To 'design' something means, according to Merriam-Webster's dictionary, *"to create, fashion, execute, or construct according to plan"* or *"to conceive and plan out in the mind"* or *"to have as a purpose"*.[14].

The assertion that the world is intelligently designed means therefore apparently something like 'The world is constructed or created according to an intelligent entity's plan'. The intelligence of this designing entity draws – ac-

---

[14] http://www.m-w.com/dictionary/design

cording to an Encyclopædia Britannica 1994-2002 definition – at least upon *"cognitive processes, such as perception, learning, memory, reasoning, and problem solving"*.

In line with his information theoretical argumentation strategy Dembski 1998 gives an etymological explanation of the adjective 'intelligent':

> The word "intelligent" derives from two Latin words, the preposition *inter*, meaning between, and the verb *lego*, meaning to choose or select. Thus according to its etymology, intelligence consists in *choosing between*. It follows that the etymology of the word "intelligent" parallels the formal analysis of intelligent causation just given. "Intelligent design" is therefore a thoroughly apt phrase, signifying that design is inferred precisely because an intelligent cause has done what only an intelligent cause can do - make a choice.[15]

There exist intelligently designed things in the world, no doubt – my alarm clock, for instance.

Why is my alarm clock intelligently designed? It is *designed* because it wouldn't exist if there hadn't been one or several persons with a plan, the will, and the possibilities to execute it. It is *intelligently* designed because its existence and the way it functions have a meaning to a certain kind of beings in the world. These are beings that divide the happenings of the world into equal parts and measure them by means of conventional units of time going by. My alarm clock is intelligently designed because it serves a purpose; it shows the time and wakes me up, if I program it to do so.

To be designed means for my alarm clock that it works as a physical thing on the one side, and according to an intelligent being's plan or program on the other side. On the physical level, it works in the same way as all other physical things do. Being designed, my alarm clock works in a different way from most of the other things in its environment and in the whole world. The most striking difference between the functioning of my alarm clock and the functioning of the majority of other things is the fact that my alarm clock, as long as it works, does the same thing all the time. It works according to a program, which prescribes how it should work. It is, one can say, *determined*.

A designed world, a world that works according to a designing entity's plan or program, is thus a determined, a deterministic world. This is also true

---

[15] Dembski (1998). See also http://www.arn.org/docs/dembski/wd_idtheory.htm.

(I think), if it would have been designed to be an evolving (emerging) world. Its evolution would in this case be predetermined.

Let us push things to the limit and imagine a world not only designed to evolve, but to evolve by chance – by accidental variations and selection of advantageous features. In this case then, I think, we have got a world designed to transcend its design, its program. Such a world would be designed to – that is, would be determined to – not to be determined: we could call it a deterministic-non-deterministic world. That would be a world that is both deterministic and non-deterministic and neither deterministic nor non-deterministic at the same time. In such a world, it should be possible to find indications for both its being designed and not being designed. The world we live in, I guess, is such a world.

Let us look at my alarm clock once again to figure out what it would mean if it were designed by its clockmaker to transcend its design. Apparently, my alarm clock would be promoted to an evolutionary being. It could learn to adapt its construction and way of functioning to changing environmental conditions. To this purpose, it should evolve sense organs, the ability of locomotion, and eventually of reproduction. In the long run the world of evolving alarm clocks would evolve to a world of, in one or other way, "living" and intelligent alarm clocks. In this world, if it still was a human world too, it is thinkable that one day my alarm clock and I could find out how to communicate with each other; I mean not only physically, but also symbolically, by means of conventional signs. If so, we could discuss, insofar as we didn't have to discuss more important things, the world's either designed or not designed construction and way of functioning, its meaningfulness or meaninglessness and so on. I could point out to the alarm clock that its ancestors a long time ago were designed by some of my ancestors to evolve into entities that transcend their original design. That is fine, could my alarm clock reply, I am thus the descendant of creatures created to be not determined by their design. It seems to me, could my alarm clock continue, we, you and me, are in the same evolutionary boat. If we are designed as beings that aren't to be determined by our design, then it really doesn't matter, if we are designed or not designed, or does it? Because our designers, though they could know that there would be a world of evolving beings couldn't know how these beings would evolve and into which kinds of beings they would evolve. On the other side, if our designers would have known in advance that we one day would be sitting here and discussing these issues they wouldn't really have designed the world as a world transcending its design, that is, as an evolutionary world. Our world would thus be a deterministic world, a world where everything that exists and happens, also evolution itself, is not the outcome of reality, that is of everything there is the case, has been the case, and will be the case, but of an all-embracing plan or program.

So my evolutionary alarm clock could speak to me, if a long, long time ago there had existed one or several alarm-clockmakers, which had designed alarm clocks as beings that were able to transcend their design.

I will now transcend these lines of thought and address the question if there is a demarcation between knowledge and belief.

5.3 My epistemological argument against intelligent design

There exist entities in the world having physical anatomies and ways of functioning that are "meaningful" in relation to their environment. We say these entities are *adapted* to their environment.

There exist intelligent entities in the world. In respect to these entities, we can say, the world is intelligent. The question is, if the existence of intelligent entities in the world is evidence for an intelligent designer of this world. How can we answer this question? Can we achieve knowledge about it?

I think it is no surprise to say that the main point in the debate between proponents and opponents of the claim that the world is intelligently designed, is the question if there is a *demarcation* between knowledge and belief, or not. The history of modern science from the Renaissance to our days is a long and stubborn fight for the conviction that there is such a demarcation. Knowledge and belief are – thus says the scientific community - not near relatives of the same epistemic family, but rather related as distant ancestor (belief) and modern descendant (knowledge-based science). Belief, the ancestor, presupposes consciousness, that is sensibility for received information, and the prerequisites of information processing, that is the ability of digitalizing or categorizing analog information. To awaken to consciousness and become able to categorize sensations is perhaps *the* biggest success of evolution – since the Big Bang, the invention of atom, and the invention of DNA. To be able to believe something one must be able mentally to constitute objects and concepts, that is to form an opinion of or find a meaning in something. And to form an opinion about objects on the basis of sensations is, I would say, the progenitor of knowledge. The modern descendant of this progenitor, scientific knowledge, is not satisfied with just forming an opinion or drafting a meaning: it also asks for *evidence* and *justification* of a person's belief that something is such and such. Knowledge, we can say, is meaning or believing something *and* trying to confirm it.

I will start my further considerations about our possibilities to know wether the world is intelligently designed or not, with a couple of truisms.

> First truism: We can only understand what we are able to understand.
> Second truism: We can't understand what we are unable to understand.
> Third truism: We can't understand more than what we are able to understand.

I will continue with the assumption that we only can understand and know something about things that are real.

A first corollary of this assumption is:

> In order to understand or know what intelligence is, we have to study the real forms of intelligence.

Second corollary:

> In order to understand or realize what design – that is planned intentional action – is, we have to study the forms of planned, intentional actions that exist in reality.

With these things in our epistemic backpack let us consider what intelligence and acting according to a plan means in reality.

What is intelligence? In accord, I hope, with the Encyclopædia Britannica's definition whereby intelligence *is not itself a cognitive or mental process, but rather a selective combination of these processes purposively directed toward effective adaptation to the environment*, I will interpret intelligence as the ability to infer from the experience of something that actually is the case, and from the reconstruction of something that earlier was the case, the possibility or probability of something that, in future, could be the case.

In other words, intelligence presupposes that there exists something that we can't know or can't know yet. Thus, real knowledge – the result of intelligent behavior – involves the possibility of ignorance. The future, whatever there will be or will happen, is not knowable to any intelligent real system or being. Real beings are just able to infer from what actually is knowable and from what actually is knowable about the past, to that which actually is more or less probable in the future.

To be able to know, presupposes thus to be able to be mistaken. Knowing presupposes the possibility of ignorance. A real system or being that on basis of the actually knowable and the former real would be able to know the future, would not really be intelligent, or, more positively formulated, would be non-real intelligent, because for such a system or being there would nothing be left to know. Reality wouldn't contain anything for which it would be worthwhile really to be intelligent – that is, intelligent in a way that can be experienced and studied in reality.

I summarize: intelligence, the striving for knowledge, presupposes real ignorance, the existence of something actually (here and now) not knowable.

Let us now look at the question what it means to plan and act according to a plan in reality.

I'll start again – not with a truism but I hope, an uncontroversial characterization of the concept of action. To act means, I suppose, that an agent, on the basis of what he or she knows about reality, causes something that wouldn't exist or be the case without his or her interference with reality.

Acting presupposes, then, not only real knowledge about but also real *interference* with reality. That means it presupposes the possibility of failure. The agent may loose interest, go mad, or become physically or mentally unable to perform the planned action. External conditions that are the really existing conditions of action at the time of the agents being prepared to act, may prevent him/her from acting. The agent has maybe based his/her intention and action plan on an erroneous view of reality.

Let me sum up again: the agent, because his or her intention does not become real by itself, has to interfere, that is get himself/herself dirty, with reality in order to act. Neither is the agent able to know or to be certain in advance that his or her action will succeed. In order to be able to act anyway, he/she has to risk that the attempt to act will go wrong or that the performed action does not result in the intended goal.

Let us now put things together and conclude what it means to act intelligently. Intelligent action, the realization of a plan, presupposes a reality in which plans and their realization can go wrong. It presupposes, thus, a reality in which not everything is the result of an in advance realized plan. Real action presupposes therefore the possibility of chance. And, what is more, in a not accidental, that is in a deterministic, world intelligent action is meaningless, since in such a world there exists nothing, nothing happens, and nothing is realizable that wouldn't also exist and happen without intelligent action.

Now, at last, I will consider the question, if there exists a demarcation between knowing and knowledge on the one side and believing and religious creed, philosophy of life or ideology on the other side.

Let us first cast a quick glance at what it means that the world has to be accidental in order to make it possible to plan and act intelligently.

To be real, that is to be the case, at least presupposes extensionality, that is either to be spatial or temporal extended or both:

1. Only what is in relation to, or separable or distinguishable from some

other thing, and only what is divisible in parts is real. The real presupposes, thus, some other real, which it can be spatially related to, extending and/or moving away from or towards it.

2. The real, strictly speaking the actually real, that which is the case here and now, presupposes too a real relationship to something no longer or not yet real being. In other words, reality presupposes real time, or the reality of time. If time only were an epistemic ordering of things, a Kantian intuition form, it wouldn't really play a role in reality. It wouldn't make a difference or have consequences, if something is the case now, has been the case earlier, or will be the case later. Only real time – only when it really makes a difference if an event is past, present or future – really matters. And the other way round: only the temporally real can really be real.

I claimed earlier that knowledge and belief are not children of the same parents. Though you could say knowing is a kind of believing, you can't put things also the other way round and claim that believing is a kind of knowing. Notwithstanding that they are epistemic relatives and do have common ancestors, there is a crucial difference: while with good reason you can conclude from *knowing* that *p* to *p being the case*, there are no good reasons to conclude from *believing* that *p* to *p being the case*. Knowing is bound or committed to the real, believing is not.

Another crucial point of difference between belief and knowledge is that, while the former can be personal or private, the latter cannot. The standard definition of knowledge, stating that it is a person's or group of persons true and justified belief or opinion about a thing, makes it clear: to believe or mean something may be – as long as it is not yet confirmed by evidence or justified by proof – personal or private. But confirming or proving it is fundamentally not private. Simply because mankind has decided to call only such procedures a confirmation or a proof that can be repeated again and again – regardless of person, place and time.

One could emphasize the crucial difference between knowledge and belief in this way: A knowledge candidate is a proposal to analyse, test or proof an assumption or system of assumptions that possibly explain a phenomenon or a set of phenomena. On the other hand, a belief candidate is a suggestion to find a meaning in the way we experience the world, be it in particular or as a whole. Knowledge is seeking confirmation of more or less general assumptions that possibly explain facts. Science, the methodical seeking of knowledge about facts, offers procedures of critically proving assumptions. Belief is seeking meaning in our experience of external facts and internal feelings. Religious creed or secular ideology doesn't want to be proved, but believed. Contrary to science it offers meaning for shared convictions. We can't know if the world as a whole has meaning, because, in order to know it, we should be able to transcend the whole world, that is the totality of spatially and temporally extended real things and events. To believe in what is impossible to know, is to believe in miracles.

5.4 The confusion of meaning and truth

Let me underpin the demarcation between knowledge and belief a little bit more by means of Searle's (2005) differentiation between "intention-with-a-t" and "intension-with-an-s". He says:

> A standard confusion in the philosophical literature is to suppose that there is some special connection between intentionality-with-a-t and intensionality-with-an-s. Some authors even allege that these are identical. But in fact the two notions are quite distinct. Intentionality-with-a-t is that property of the mind by which it is directed at, or is about objects and states of affairs in the world. Intensionality-with-an-s is that phenomenon by which sentences fail certain tests for extensionality. (ibid., 385)

Searle has here two tests in mind, the one based on Leibniz's law of the substitutability of identicals, the other based on the principle of existential inference. For our purpose it suffices to deal with the latter. The principle *"states that any statement which contains a referring expression implies the existence of the object referred to by that expression"* (ibid.). For instance, from the statement

'Astrid believes that God created the world'

it does not follow that

'There is some x such that Astrid believes x created the world'.

The relation between intensionality-with-an-s and intentionality-with-a-t is based on the fact that sentences that are intensional-with-an-s are about states of mind that are intentional-with-a-t (cf. ibid.). In consequence the truth conditions of such sentences *"do not require that the world be as represented by the original intentional states, but only that the content of the intentional state be as represented in the sentences about those intentional states"* (ibid., 385-386).

Looking back at Kant's 1762 handling of modalities and their role for propositional content, i.e. for what Frege called 'Sinn' and what later on came to be named 'intension', it becomes clear that the intentionality-with-a-t of our states of mind is only a part of and embedded in a more comprehensive relationship between the subjective mind, the world, and other minds. I will call this relationship a *communication environment* and claim that intentional states are always at the same time intensional states relative to a certain (or several) communication environments. In consequence, all sentences expressing an intentional state can be translated into intensional sentences explicating not only the propositional content but also the intentional state of the uttering mind and (at least implicitly) the specification of the communication environment in which the state of mind and/or its expression takes place. It is the – cultural, social, and historical specified – communication environment that is responsible for the meaning and truth criteria that guide and control the processes of meaning construction and communication taking place within the environment.

When, for instance, Anselm calls God *"that than which no greater can be conceived"*, the propositional content 'God is that than which no greater can be conceived' is an abridged version of the more explicative intensional form 'Anselm believes that God is that than which no grater can be conceived'. This form again can be made more explicit yet by 'Anselm believes as a prominent member of the medieval, catholic, philosophic-theological research community and communication environment that God is that ...'.

If we don't want to believe in a miraculous attuning between states of our own mind and other minds and states of the world, we – as members of and communicators within a communication environment – are obliged to understand, follow and, if necessary, develop on the basis of new experiences those validity rules that guide and control the processes of meaning constitution and communication within the environment.

As Kant 1762 (1916) and 1998 made very clear, with the development of modern science there evolved a communication environment that obliges/constrains the truthfulness of intentional states of mind to experience and the meaningfulness of reasoning to validity rules of inference. To believe – as earlier proponents of ontological or cosmological proofs of a transcendent divine world-creator did and today's proponents of cosmological proofs of a transcendent divine world-designer do – that the propositional content of a state of mind or its semiotic expression in a sentence, a picture or whatever by itself can prove its truth, is a breach of the basic rules of truthfulness and validity of a scientific, knowledge-obliged communication environment[16]. If we are ready to infer existence from possibility, we believe that our meaningful, i.e. intensional-with-an-s, considerations are by themselves able to imply the truth of their propositional content. In other words, we believe that our intensional-with-an-s statements stand the test of existential inference.

Let me conclude my considerations about the dangers of confusing intentionality-with-a-t with intensionality-with-an-s by citing Searle's 2005 words:

> The truth conditions of these intensional-with-an-s sentences do not require that the world be as represented by the original intentional states, but only that the content of the intentional state be as represented in the sentences about those intentional states. Since intentional-with-a-t states are representations, and since the content of the representation can be reported independently of whether or not it is satisfied, or even independently of whether or not the objects purportedly referred to by the representation even exist, the report of the intentional state does not commit the person making the report to the existence of the objects referred to by the original representation (existential generalization). (ibidem, 385-386)

The explanation for the failure of the test is according to Searle (2005) *"that the ground floor intentional states in the minds ... are representations, but their reports in sentences ... are representations of representations"* (ibid., 386). Searle continues:

> The truth of the representation of the representation depends *not* on how things are in the real world represented by the original intentional representation (the original intentional state), but rather,

---

[16]Questions of the validity of our knowledge belong to the descriptive or factual as well as to the normative side of knowledge generating processes. I agree with Piaget (1970) and Brandom (1994) that there is no principal *"separation of norm and fact"* (cf. Piaget (1970, p. 4)). Factual or descriptive knowledge is always bound up with and relative to a system of norms guiding knowledge generating processes within a certain communication environment. These norms, however, are to be understood as being nothing else than successful experiences transformed into prescriptive actions, i.e. research methods.

how they are in the mental world of that intentional representation. And that mental representation can be reported accurately even though the objects purportedly referred to by that representation do not exist. (ibid.)

Let us have a final look at Kant's 1762 considerations of *the only possible argument for the demonstration of the existence of God*. He divides all possible arguments for the existence of a divine entity into logical or possibility arguments and empirical or existential arguments (cf. 1916, 223). The first ones are arguments on the basis of understanding concepts, the latter are arguments on the basis of empirical concepts. There are two kinds of logical arguments – the ontological and the cosmological. As explained in the first paragraph of this paper, Kant 1998 rejects the ontological and accepts – as reasonable but not sound – the cosmological argument.

There are also two possible empirical arguments. The first infers from empirical evidence of a divine ordering of nature onto the existence of an independent cause of the world. It follows then from the conceptual content of such an independent cause that it is of divine nature. Kant 1762 rejects this argument since in its second step boils it down to the ontological argument. The other type of empirical argument infers from empirical evidence directly onto the existence and the divine properties of a first cause. This argument, though not sound either, is according to Kant 1762 *"not only possible but deserves in every respect through common efforts to be completed"* (ibid., 227-228, my transl.). Kant continues:

> The things of the world that reveal themselves for our senses show distinct features of their contingency as well as through their magnitude, ordering and suitable design that one is able to discover everywhere evidence of a reasonable creator of great wisdom, power, and goodness. (ibid., 228, my transl.)

This argument, though lacking, according to Kant, "geometrical strength", resembles the argumentation of today's ID-proponents, who claim to be able to demonstrate the existence of a divine creator on the basis of empirical evidence. Nevertheless, neither a whole universe of empirical evidence of *complex specified informational* (Dembski 1998) and material structures could compensate for the simple fact that neither logical inference nor direct experience can demonstrate the existence of a transcendent divine entity.

Let me sum up: I hope I have been fairly successful in constructing my metaphysical and my epistemological argument such that they support my final conclusion as follows:

Whether the world is intelligently designed or not, we cannot know – neither by our knowledge about the world nor by our knowledge about what it means to believe or to know something. However, whether or not a person or a communication environment of like-minded people chooses to believe it, that is another point altogether.

Chapter 6

Evolution, Intelligent Design and the re-emergence of Militant Atheism

Søren Holm[1]

Professor Søren Holm	Or	Professor Søren Holm
Cardiff Law School		Section for Medical Ethics
Museum Avenue		Fredrik Holsts Hus
Cardiff		Ullevål Terrasse
CF10 3XJ		Pb. 1130 Blindern
UK		N-0318 Oslo
		NORWAY

"I think that you and Richard are absolute disasters in the fight against intelligent design – we are losing this battle, not the least of which is the two new supreme court justices who are certainly going to vote to let it into classrooms – what we need is not knee-

---

[1] This paper was mainly written before the publication of Dawkins' book "The God Delusion" Dawkins (2006), but after the screening in the UK of the two strongly anti-theistic television programs "The Root of all Evil?" to which the book is linked. This is the reason that this paper only contains very few quotations from that book. In revising the paper for publication I have studied the book and found it to be even more virulently anti-theistic than Dennett's book, and considerably less argued, but then Dawkins is a scientist and not a philosopher.

jerk atheism but serious grappling with the issues – neither of you are willing to study Christianity seriously and to engage with the ideas – it is just plain silly and grotesquely immoral to claim that Christianity is simply a force for evil, as Richard claims – more than this, we are in a fight, and we need to make allies in the fight, not simply alienate everyone of good will."[2]

There is an old link between evolutionary theory and militant atheism[3] that we can trace all the way back to Thomas Huxley, famously nicknamed "Darwin's Bulldog"[4]. The core idea is simply that the fact of evolution makes belief in religion impossible, or more succinctly that evolutionary theory implies atheism[5]. The intermediary premises in the argument from "Evolution is a fact" to "Belief in religion is impossible (or intellectually unsustainable)" vary. The traditional target of this line of argument was Christianity, partly because Christianity was the religion of the West, partly because some evolutionary theorists also held a rather vulgar social evolutionary theory of religion that placed monotheism in general and Christianity in particular as the pinnacle of religious evolution. Recently an attack has been made on all religious belief by prominent protagonists of evolutionary theory. Richard Dawkins and Daniel Dennett have, as far as I am aware somewhat independently, launched ferocious attacks on all kinds of religion[6].

In this paper I will consider the Dawkins and Dennett arguments, and show that they actualise the very same tensions between science and belief that are actualised by the controversy concerning Intelligent Design (ID).

---

[2]From an e-mail from Michael Ruse to Daniel Dennett, February 19 2006, available at http://www.uncommondescent.com/index.php/archives/844.

[3]By "militant atheism" I mean any atheistic view which actively attempts to "convert" theists, *and* which (partly) attempts to achieve this conversion by a denigration of their religious beliefs.

[4]Huxley invented the word "agnostic" (see the Oxford English Dictionary entry for "agnostic") and claimed to be one, but there is little difference between his concept of agnosticism and atheism.

[5]This is a specific variant of the more general argumentative move that scientific finding X makes religious belief R impossible and that the conjunction of all scientific findings X_n, makes any and all religious beliefs R_n imposssible

[6]Dennett (2006).

6.1 The Dawkins and Dennett arguments

The arguments put forward by Dawkins and Dennett are not perfectly identical[7]. There are subtle differences, but the main argument is the same and proceeds as follows:

1. The emergence of religious memes (i.e. religious ideas and beliefs) can be fully explained by evolutionary influences on early modern man[8]

2. The further spread, development and fixation of religious memes can be fully explained by evolutionary memetics

3. All religions are therefore 100% natural phenomena

4. It can be shown that religious memes are deleterious for the organisms / humans that harbour them and that they should therefore be classified as parasites

5. From 3 it follows that the religious explanation of religions is false (i.e. if religions are 100% natural phenomena, none of them are the result of Divine revelation)

6. From 4 and 5 it follows that there is reason to attempt to eradicate religions and religious beliefs, that everyone who has religious beliefs suffer from false consciousness, and that there is no reason not to attempt to eradicate religious belief.

There are a number of problems with this argument that are worth mentioning, if only in passing. The first is that both Dawkins and Dennett relies on Dawkins' concept of memes, i.e. beliefs and practices that propagate themselves culturally, but are subject to evolution in the sense that memes only survive and spread if they manage to propagate themselves to new minds. The whole "science" of memetics is hugely contested partly because it essentially relies on Larmarckian transmission of memetic information in contrast to the Darwinian transmission of genetic information, partly because the individuation of memes is problematic.

---

[7]Dawkins and Dennett consider a range of other arguments for and against religion, for instance concerning the plausibility of certain conceptualisations of the deity or of the possibility of divine intervention in the world, but their distinctive contribution (if any) is the evolutionary argument. The other anti-theistic arguments can be found far back in the history of philosophy.

[8]Note that the argument has no probative force against a believer in so-called "theistic evolution" since 1. is fully compatible with the belief that the evolutionary forces and the substrate on which they worked where guided and designed by the deity.

Second, the move from 1 & 2 to 3 is problematic in two ways. It may be possible to plot a plausible history for the natural development of religion (as in 1 & 2), but that only leads to 3 being plausible and not certain. And, importantly most religious people would not be resistant to 1 & 2 if "fully" was exchanged for "somewhat".

Third, establishing 4 is far beyond the skills of Dawkins and Dennett. Dawkins make a particularly bad stab at this in his essay "Time to stand up", where he argues that not only is religion responsible for the September 11, 2001 attacks on the USA, but more generally for most wars and conflicts ever:

> 'The bitter hatreds that now poison Middle Eastern politics are rooted in the real or perceived wrong of the setting up of a Jewish State in an Islamic region.
>
> [...]
>
> I do not intend to get into that argument. But if it had not been for religion, the very concept of a Jewish State would have had no meaning in the first place. Nor would the very concept of Islamic lands, as something to be invaded and desecrated. In a world without religion, there would have been no Crusades; no Inquisition; no anti-Semitic pogroms (the people of the diaspora would long ago have intermarried and become indistinguishable from their host populations); no Northern Ireland Troubles (no label by which to distinguish the two 'communities', and no sectarian schools to teach the children historic hatreds — they would simply be one community.)' [9]

Are we really to believe that all, or even most of the wars in Europe and the Middle East in the Middle Ages would not have happened if there had been no religions. Is it not plausible that the ambitions of the various kings and princes would have lead to wars, whether or not these wars could have been given a religious justification[10]? And for later wars it seems wholly implausible to even try to mount a claim that the first and second world war were in any significant sense religious wars. True, states used religion to bolster the fighting spirit ("Gott mit Uns" on the belt buckles of German soldiers, military chaplains in every army and the ubiquitous presence of religious imagery), but the wars

---

[9] Dawkins (2004, p. 188).

[10] Note for instance the minimal role of religion in the fourth crusade.

were not caused by, or significantly sustained by religion[11,12].

Dawkins tries to answer these kinds of arguments slightly earlier in the same essay where he writes:

> 'My point is not that religion itself is the motivation for wars, murders and terrorist attacks, but that religion is the principal label, and the most dangerous one, by which a 'they' as opposed to a 'we' can be identified at all. I am not even claiming that religion is the only label by which we identify the victims of our prejudice. There's also skin colour, language, and social class. But often, as in Northern Ireland, these don't apply and religion is the only divisive label around. Even when it is not alone, religion is nearly always an incendiary ingredient in the mix as well.'[13]

The last sentence is essentially an immunisation strategy against possible counterexamples and need not detain us more here, but the previously introduced distinction between religion as the motivation for war and religion as a possible label by which to establish an in- and an out-group is interesting. Primarily because it actually seems to work against Dawkins' stated argument. If the motivation for conflict is not religious (as per Dawkins' distinction), but some real or imagined underlying non-religious grievance it seems even more implausible to claim that most conflicts would not happen if we just abolished religion.

Fourth, we might have reason to worry about the deflationary potential of D&Ds line of argument. If the argument goes through for 1-3 and if 5 & 6 follow from 1-3 and 4 religion and religious beliefs may just be a placeholder for many other "memes" to which we have become attached (or on the D&D theory that have attached themselves to us). Can we really be certain that most of ethics, including altruism, beneficence and justice, is not explained away by this argument scheme?

Fifth, and finally we might note that a completely parallel argument can be mounted against "rational atheism", i.e. the belief that it is rational to be an atheist (see the footnote for this argument), and D&D's argument is thus

---

[11] The origins of the first world war can probably with equal justification be traced to a particular version of Social Darwinism emphasising the competition between societies for resources and colonies.

[12] For a serious attempt to answer the question whether Christianity in particular causes wars see Martin (1998).

[13] Dawkins (2004, p. 187).

potentially destructive of their own belief in rational atheism[14]. D&D could argue that although the acceptance of the evolutionary meme is a result of evolutionary memetics, the justification or epistemic warrant of this meme is independent of its origin. What justifies belief in evolution is rational thought and evidence. But as soon as that move is made it is 1) obvious that exactly the same move can be made by the religious believer, and that 3 no longer implies 5, and 2) that the problem only moves one step back to the justification of the "high valuation of rationality" meme.

6.2 The intellectual *superbia* of Dawkins and Dennett

In passing we might note a certain amount of intellectual *superbia*[15] and lack of sophistication in the writings of Dawkins and Dennett. The *superbia* can be found in Dennett's statement that:

> 'I for one am not in awe of your faith. I am appalled by your arrogance, by your unreasonable certainty that you have all the answers. I wonder if any believers in the End Times will have the intellectual honesty and courage to read this book through.'[16]

---

[14]

1. The emergence of atheist memes (i.e. atheist ideas and beliefs) can be fully explained by evolutionary influences on early modern man

2. The further spread, development and fixation of atheist memes can be fully explained by evolutionary memetics

3. Atheism is therefore a 100% natural phenomena

4. It can be shown that atheist memes are deleterious for the organisms / humans that harbour them and that they should therefore be classified as parasites

5. From 3 it follows that the atheist explanation of atheist beliefs is false (i.e. if atheism is a 100% natural phenomenon, it is not based on rational thought)

6. From 4 and 5 it follows that there is reason to attempt to eradicate atheism and atheistic beliefs, that everyone who has atheist beliefs suffer from false consciousness, and that there is no reason not to attempt to eradicate atheist belief.

[15] Superbia is one of the 7 cardinal sins and is traditionally translated from the Latin as "pride", but a better translation is probably "Too high an estimation of yourself".

[16] Dennett (2006, p. 51).

Dennett's doubts about the honesty and courage of his opponents loses something of its rhetorical force by being placed on page 51, since only those who have already suffered 50 pages of Dennett's prose will ever realise what he really thinks about them. Why not put this on the cover of the book?

And in Dawkin's publicly stated refusal to discuss with creationists, because he thinks that *his* taking part in such discussions adds to the legitimacy of creationism:

> 'Ever since that phone call, I have repeatedly cited you and refused to debate these people, not because I am afraid of 'losing' the debate, but because, as you said, just to appear on a platform with them is to lend them the respectability they Crave.'[17]

I do not for a moment doubt that both Dawkins and Dennett are highly intelligent and accomplished, but so are many academics and other people that hold religious beliefs (it would for instance be extremely difficult to claim that the current Archbishop of Canterbury, Rowan Williams or the current Pope Benedict the XVIth are not first rate academics, as are many religious critics of evolution). D&D's superbia therefore seems very badly placed. This is especially the case because their own understanding of religion and theology is rather deficient[18].

6.3 Intelligent Design and religious belief

In discussions about ID arguments are often put forward linking the validity of ID as a research program or theory with the religious beliefs of ID proponents. But such arguments are clearly *non sequiturs* and examples of classic argumentative errors. Depending on the way in which they are formulated these arguments against ID are either examples of *ad hominem* arguments or examples of *poisoning the well* arguments. The fact that someone holds religious beliefs has no direct bearing on whether a scientific proposition they have put forward is true, plausible, verisimilar or falsifiable.

A typical example of the anti-ID rhetoric can be found in an article written by Richard Dawkins and Jerry Coyne in the British newspaper The Guardian:

> Intelligent design is not an argument of the same character as these controversies. It is not a scientific argument at all, but a religious one. It might be worth discussing in a class on the history of ideas, in a philosophy class on popular logical fallacies, or in a comparative religion class on origin myths from around the world. But it no more belongs in a biology class than alchemy belongs in

---

[17]Dawkins (2004, p. 257).
[18]See for instance McGrath (2004).

a chemistry class, phlogiston in a physics class or the stork theory in a sex education class. In those cases, the demand for equal time for "both theories" would be ludicrous. Similarly, in a class on 20th-century European history, who would demand equal time for the theory that the Holocaust never happened?"[19]

The debate about ID is complicated by the fact that three separate issues are often confounded, especially in the USA from which much of the ID debate is transferred rather uncritically to Europe:

1. Is ID a (currently[20]) sustainable scientific hypothesis or research program?

2. Should ID be taught (or even mentioned) in schools? (and if so in what part of the curriculum)

3. Should ID be taught in schools as equally plausible as evolutionary theory?

I have nothing very useful to say about the first of this issue, partly because it is a scientific question better answered by biological scientists (and preferably by biological scientists who have no stake invested in the answer), partly because it is one of the questions that are most reliably answered retrospectively. In the future we will be much better able to judge whether the ID research program has produced important new research results than we are now.

The answer to 1 might, however be "Yes" and the answers to 2 and 3, or to 3 alone still be "No" and maybe the link between ID and religion could be relevant in this context. And in the USA the link is possibly relevant because of the particular way the American constitutional separation between church and state is interpreted. In American jurisprudence it would be enough to disqualify ID in state schools if ID was only held by religious people, but that is because the state cannot be *perceived* to promote any religion, not because any religion will necessarily be promoted by allowing ID some room in the curriculum. But that particular American argument is of limited relevance in contexts where there is either an established religion, or no established religion but no religion / state separation either.

---

[19] Dawkins and Coyne (2005).
The strength of Dawkins' feelings about ID can clearly be seen in his implied parallel to Holocaust denial.

[20] The "currently" is added here because it might be the case that some future scientific finding would make ID unsustainable.

Is there a more general principle that can be used to exclude ID completely from schools, or to define its place *vis a vis* evolutionary theory? A class of arguments centre on the status of ID claiming that it is either false, unsupported, implausible or problematically biased[21]. Let us for the sake of argument assume that these claims about ID are accurate. Is this enough to exclude ID from all schools, or from state supported schools?

Let us deal with the falsity claim first. If ID could be shown convincingly to be false, it should not be taught, except perhaps as part of a history of ideas curriculum as mentioned by Dawkins and Coyne. But assuming that ID is false and basing our educational argument on that assumption is just begging the central question in the debate between ID and evolutionary theory. We might also note that much of what is taught in science classes in schools is not strictly true, either because it is obsolete or because it is only the closest approximation to the truth that students (and teachers) are believed to be able to understand. But this is of course not determinative in the present case.

So let us consider a thought experiment as far removed from the evolution / ID controversy as possible, to get a better handle on the problem of teaching potentially biased subject matter in schools.

Let us imagine a school in Denmark wanting to teach a Swedophilic version of Danish history[22]. All periods of Danish history would be covered to the same extent and in the same detail as in any other Danish school, but they would all be seen from a Swedish perspective. Christian the Second would always be mentioned as "Christian the Tyrant" and not as "Christian the peasant lover", the fact that the Swedish army did not conquer Copenhagen in 1659 would be a course for lament as the beginning of the end for Sweden's ambitions as a Baltic power and not for rejoicing as the salvation of Denmark as an independent state, and the persons who rose up against the proper authorities on the Baltic island of Bornholm after its conquest by the Swedes would quite properly be described as "terrorists" and not as "good Danish men". Should the school be prevented from teaching history in this way, just because we all now that this is a false account of history (or at least all Danes know this)?

It is not clear to me that a school should be prevented from teaching Swedophilic history in this way, there is after all many schools in Sweden who teach history from this perspective without apparent harmful effects on the students (apart from turning them into Swedophiles)[23]. And if the teaching

---

[21] We might note that the bias problem occurs across the curriculum and with particular force in the social sciences where all accounts of society are to some degree infected by ideology.

[22] For readers outside of Scandinavia I should point out that Sweden and Denmark are, and always have been neighbours and that Sweden is "the traditional enemy" of Denmark.

[23] Or, perhaps more accurately there were schools in Sweden who taught in this way before

was not a 100% Swedophilic approach but was truly balanced by a Danophilic approach taught with the same conviction, it would be even more difficult to say that such teaching should be prohibited. We may of course doubt whether a committed swedophilic teacher can teach danophilic history (or *vice versa*), but that worry does not matter to the same degree if the question is not about the specific delivery, but about the allowability of a specific approach as part of a curriculum.

There is bound to be disagreement about how close the analogy is between teaching ID and teaching Swedophilic history, but even if the analogy is not perfect it at least shows that teaching ID as part of a broad biology curriculum cannot be claimed to be highly problematic.

6.4 Turning the table

What would happen if we apply the standards proposed by ID opponents to Dawkins' and Dennett's anti-theistic arguments?

Well, it was clear long before the specific arguments mentioned here were put forward that D&D were not just atheists, but anti-theists. They were not only non-believers, but they believed that religious belief was foolish, intellectually unsound and harmful to societies and individuals.

If the prior beliefs of a non-scientific nature of the proponents are important for the evaluation of scientific arguments, then it seems to follow straightforwardly that D&D's arguments are tarred with exactly the same brush they and others use to tar ID. They are just as infested with prior problematic belief.

D&D might of course reply that their prior beliefs are irrelevant to the assessment of the validity of their arguments, because their prior beliefs are scientific and therefore different from the prior beliefs of religious ID proponents. But that argument is clearly circular. It is only if their argument succeeds that their prior beliefs are vindicated as (more) scientific.[24] And we might, furthermore suspect that their anti-theism has very little to do with science, since it is so vehemently held. To Dawkins and Dennett the non-existence of God, and the, to them lamentable existence of God, religions and religious people is not a trivial matter as exemplified in a quote from "The God Delusion":

> "The God of the Old Testament is arguably the most unpleasant character in all fiction: jealous and proud of it; a petty, unjust, un-

---

we all become terribly worried about being nice to our neighbours and giving a "balanced" account of history.

[24]The same is true to some degree for ID. If ID is vindicated one of the perceived obstacles to religious belief is removed.

forgiving control-freak; a vindictive, bloodthirsty ethnic cleanser; a misogynistic, homophobic, racist, infanticidal, genocidal, filicidal, pestilential, megalomaniacal, sadomasochistic, capriciously malevolent bully."[25]

6.5 Conclusion

In this paper I have argued for three conclusions: 1) that the resurgence of militant atheism or anti-theism among evolutionary theorists rests on problematic arguments, 2) that if the the anti-religious arguments of the self-same evolutionary theorists against Intelligent Design are taken seriously, they also casts doubt on their own evolution-based anti-theistic arguments, and 3) that the standard arguments against the teaching of ID in schools are weak.

If this is right one can only hope that more moderate voices on both sides of the science-religion debate will find the courage to continue their engagement in honest academic debate, despite the interventions of the militant atheists.

---

[25]Dawkins (2006, p. 31).

Bibliography

Andriesse, C. and Hollestelle, M.: 2001, Minimum entropy production in photosynthesis, *Biophys. Chem.* **90**, 249–253.

Aristotle: n.d., Eudemian ethics, http://www.perseus.tufts.edu/cgi-bin/ptext?lookup=Aristot.+Eud.+Eth.+8.1248a.

Barrow, J. D. and Tipler, F. J.: 1986, *The Anthropic Cosmological Principle*, Oxford University Press.

Bear, J.: 1972, *Dynamics of Fluids in Porous Media*, American Elsevier, New York.

Behe, M. J.: 1996, *Darwin's Black Box*, The Free Press, New York.

Behe, M. J.: 2007, *The Edge of Evolution: The Search for the Limits of Darwinism*, The Free Press.

Bohn, S., Andreotti, B., Douady, S., Munzinger, J. and Couder, Y.: 2002, Constitutive property of the local organization of leaf venation networks, *Physical Review* **E65**. 061914.

Bossard, D. C.: 2005, The rise and fall of scientific naturalism, *Research Report 55*, IBRI. http://www.ibri.org/DVD-1/RRs/RR055/SciNat.html.

Bourke, V. J.: 1967, St. thomas aquinas, *The Encyclopedia of Philosophy*, Vol. 8, Collier Macmillan Publishers, pp. 105–116.

Brandom, R.: 1994, *Making it Explicit*, Harvard University Press, Cambridge, Massachusetts, London.

Caspar, M. and Dyck, W. v.: 1930, *Johannes Kepler in seinen Briefen*, R. Oldenbourg, Munich and Berlin.

Cochard, H., Nardini, A. and Coll, L.: 2004, Hydraulic architecture of leaf blades: where is the main resistance?, *Plant, Cell and Environment* **27**, 1257–67.

Davies, P.: 1988, *The Cosmic Blueprint*, Templeton Foundation.

Davies, P.: 2006, *The Goldilocks Enigma*, Allen Lane.

Dawkins, R.: 2004, *A Devil's Chaplain*, Phoenix, London.

Dawkins, R.: 2006, *The God Delusion*, Bantam Press.

Dawkins, R. and Coyne, J.: 2005, One side can be wrong, The Guardian, September 1, 2005 (education section).

Dembski, W. A.: 1998, Intelligent design as a theory of information, http://www.arn.org/docs/dembski/wd_idtheory.htm.

Dembski, W. A.: 2004, *The Design Revolution – Answering the Toughest Questions About Intelligent Design*, InterVarsity Press.

Dennett, D.: 2006, *Breaking the Spell: Religion as a Natural Phenomenon*, Penguin, London.

Drake, S.: 1957, *Discoveries and opinions of Galileo*, Doubleday & Company, New York.

Encyclopædia Britannica, Deluxe Millennium Second Edition: 1994-2002, CD-ROM.

Flew, A. and Habermas, G. R.: 2005, My pilgrimage from atheism to theism: An exclusive interview with former british atheist professor antony flew, *Philosophia Christi* **7**(2).

Gingerich, O.: 1994, Dare a scientist believe in design?, *in* J. M. Templeton (ed.), *Evidence of Purpose*, Continuum, New York, pp. 21–32.

Gonzalez, G. and Richards, J.: 2004, *The Privileged Planet: How Our Place in the Cosmos is Designed for Discovery*, Regnery Publishing, Washington DC.

Hawking, S.: 1998, *Eine kurze Geschichte der Zeit*, Rowohlt, Reinbek b. Hamburg.

Hoyle, F.: 1982, The universe: Past and present reflections, *Annual Review of Astronomy and Astrophysics* **20**, 1–35.

Jaspers, K.: 1935, *Vernunft und Existenz*, J.B. Wolters Verlag.

Kang, J. and Dengler, N.: 2004, Vein pattern development in adult leaves of arabidopsis thaliana, *Int. Journal of Plant Sciences* **165**, 231–242.

Kant, I.: 1762, Der einzig mögliche Beweisgrund zu einer Demonstration des Daseins Gottes, *Kleinere philosophische Schriften*, Insel Verlag, Leipzig. 1916.

Kant, I.: 1998, *Kritik der reinen Vernunft*, Meiner, Hamburg.

Kaplan, W.: 1991, *Advanced Calculus*, 4th edn, Addison-Wesley, Reading, MA.

Lowell, P.: 1910, *Mars as the Abode of Life*, MacMillan.

Łukasiewicz, J.: 1970, *Selected Works*, North Holland. Borkowski, L. (ed.).

Martin, D.: 1998, *Does Christianity cause wars?*, Oxford University Press.

McGee, B. (ed.): 1978, *Men of Ideas*, BBC, London.

McGrath, A.: 2004, *Dawkins' God*, Blackwell, Oxford.

Meinhardt, H.: 1976, Morphogenesis of lines and nests, *Differentiation* **6**, 117–123.

Meinhardt, H.: 1982, *Models of Biological Pattern Formation*, Academic Press, London. See also his online presentation at http://www.biologie.uni-hamburg.de/b-online/e28_1/pattern.htm.

Merriam-Webster Online: n.d., http://www.m-w.com/. Access Online August 2007.

Meyer, S. C.: 2004, Dna and the origin of life: Information, specification, and explanation, *in* J. A. Campbell and S. C. Meyer (eds), *Darwinism, Design and Public Education*, Michigan State University Press, Lansing, pp. 223–285.

Mitchison, G.: 1980, A model for vein formation in higher plants, *Proc. Royal Soc. London* **B207**, 79–109.

Monod, J.: 1971, *Chance and Necessity: An Essay on the Natural Philosophy of Modern Biology*, Alfred A. Knopf, New York.

Nancy, R.: 1998, 'You guys lost'. Is Design a closed issue?, *in* W. A. Dembski (ed.), *Mere Creation*, InterVarsity Press, pp. 73–92. p. 84.

Needham, J.: 1969, *The Grand Titration. Science and Society in East and West*, Pearcey.

O'Hara, D.: forthcoming, Peirce: Plato, miracles and the logic of history, *in* C. Pearson (ed.), *Studies in the Religious Writings of Charles S. Peirce*, Legas Press. Preprint 2006.

Øhrstrøm, P. (ed.): 2003, *Time, Reality, and Transcendence in Rational Perspective*, Aalborg University Press.

Pack, D. C.: n.d., Does God exist?, http://www.thercg.org/books/dge.html.

Passmore, J.: 1961, The 'two worlds' argument, *Philosophical Reasoning*, Charles Scribner's Sons, New York, pp. 38–67.

Peirce, C.: 1965, *Collected Papers*, Harvard University Press, Cambridge, Massachusetts. Hartshorne, Charles and Weiss, Paul (eds.).

Perez, J.-P.: 2000, Thermodynamic interpretation of the variational maxwell theorem in dc circuits, *American Journal of Physics* **68**, 860–3.

Piaget, J.: 1970, *Genetic Epistemology*, Columbia University Press, New York, London.

Plato: n.d., Theaetetus. Many editions available, also on the Internet. Any Internet search will come up with several, e.g. from Perseus.

Polanyi, M.: 1967, Life transcending physics and chemistry, *Chemical and Engineering News* pp. 54–56.

Polanyi, M.: 1968, Life's irreducible structure, *Science* **160**, 1308–12.

Pope Benedict XVI: 2006, 'Faith, Reason and the University. Memories and Reflections', Lecture of the Holy Father, 12 September 2006, University of Regensburg, Libreria Editrice Vaticana.

Popper, K. R.: 1945, *The open Society and its Enemies*, Routledge, London.

Popper, K. R.: 1972, *Objective Knowledge: An evolutionary approach*, Clarendon Press, Oxford.

Prigogine, I.: 1967, *Thermodynamics of Irreversible Processes*, Interscience, New York.

Ratzsch, D.: 2001, *Nature, Design and Science. The Status of Design in Natural Science*, State University of New York Press.

Ruse, M.: 2006, Email from michael ruse to daniel dennett, february 19, 2006, available at http://www.uncommondescent.com/index.php/archives/844.

Sack, L. and Holbrook, N.: 2006, Leaf hydraulics, *Annual Review of Plant Biology* **57**, 361–81.

Sagan, C.: 1993, *Cosmos*, Ballantine Books, New York.

Schönfeld, M.: 2003, Kant's philosophical development, Stanford Encyclopedia of Philosophy. http://plato.stanford.edu/entries/kant-development.

Searle, J.: 2005, Intentionality, *in* S. Guttenplan (ed.), *A Companion to the Philosophy of Mind*, Blackwell Publishing, Oxford.

Simpson, G.: 1953, *The Meaning of Evolution*, mentor book edn, New American Library, New York.

Sutcliffe, J.: 1968, *Plants and Water*, Edward Arnold, London.

Thaxton, C., Bradley, W. and Olsen, R.: 1984, *The Mystery of Life's Origins*, Philosophical Library, New York.

Thorvaldsen, S.: 2003, Kepler, Galileo, Newton and the constructive ideas of modern science, *in* Øhrstrøm (2003), pp. 11–38.

Turing, A.: 1952, The chemical basis of morphogenesis, *Philos. Trans. Royal Soc. London* **B237**, 37–72.

Tyvand, P.: 1982, A hydrodynamic leaf model, *Annals of Botany* **50**, 799–816.

van Till, H. J.: 2003, Intelligent design, *The Encyclopedia of Science and Religion*, Vol. 1, Thomson & Gale.

Ward, P. and Brownlee, D.: 2000, *Rare Earth: Why Complex Life is Uncommon in the Universe*, Springer, New York.

Wegener, M.: 2003, God, time & creation: An essay in metaphysics, *in* Øhrstrøm (2003), pp. 75–89.

Wells, J.: 2000, *Icons of Evolution*, Regnery Press, Washington DC.

Willmer, C. M. and Fricker, M.: 1996, *Stomata*, 2nd edn, Chapman and Hall, London.

Wittgenstein, L.: 1922, *Tractatus Logico-Philosophicus*, Routledge & Kegan-Paul. Translated from the German by C.K. Ogden, with assistance from G.E. Moore, F.P. Ramsey, and L. Wittgenstein.

Wolfram, S.: 2002, *A new kind of science*, Wolfram Media.

Yockey, H. P.: 2005, *Information theory, evolution, and the origin of life*, Cambridge University Press.

Zwieniecki, M., Melcher, P., Boyce, C.K. Sack, L. and Holbrook, N.: 2002, Hydraulic architecture of leaf venation in laurus nobilis l, *Plant, Cell and Environment* **25**, 1445–50.